Jews and Native Americans

New Relationships in a New World

Published by

Cooweescoowee Publishers LLC

15205 E Powder Dr Claremore OK 74017

Questions, comments, or perspectives can be sent to the author at Cssewell71@gmail.com.

ISBN: 978-1-329-79797-0

1. History 2. Native American 3. Oklahoma

First Edition

Printed in USA

By Hodalee C. Scott Sewell (most available on Amazon)

The Indians of North Florida: From Carolina to Florida, the Story of the Survival of a Distinct American Indian Community (2011; with S. Pony Hill)

Belles of the Creek Nation (2015)

The Cherokee Paradox: Unexpected Ancestry at the Cross-roads of Identity and Genetics (2016)

Indians of Alabama: Guide to the Indian Tribes of the Yellowhammer State (2016)

We Will Always Be Here: Native Peoples on Living and Thriving in the South (Anthology, 2016)

Redbone Chronicles (Anthology, 2016)

The Red Road: Language, Legends, and Lifeways of the Cheraw, Keyauwee, Pee Dee, San-tee & Wateree (2017; with S. Pony Hill)

The Sewell Legacy (2017)

A Type of People: The Native American Heritage of Holmes County, Florida (Aug 29, 2017 with S. Pony Hill)

Este Maskoke Em Oponvkv (2018)

Creek Indian Recipes Maskoke Country Cookin' (2018)

By S. Pony Hill (most available on Amazon)

Strangers in Their Own Land: South Carolina's State Indian Tribes (Jul 21, 2011)

Horizon - Broken Sky Paperback (May 1, 2015)

A Wandering Tribe: Dispersal of the Catawba Nation 1800 to 1900 (2018)

Contents

Introduction

In 1585, Joachim Gaunse (or Ganz) landed on Roanoke Island, becoming the first known Jew to set foot in what is today the United States, but he would be followed soon after by a steady stream of Jews arriving in the wilds of North America, seeking their fortunes and fleeing persecution in many cases. Most would meet, and many would establish relationships with, Native American individuals and communities. Across the Americas, Jews still reeling from the expulsions from Spain and the dangers of the Inquisition found the "New World" to be fertile ground for their interests, economic and religious; Jews were swift in settling in many of the West Indian colonies[1].

In 1654, the Dutch granted civil rights to the Jews of Guiana. That document began, *"To the People of the Hebrew nation that are to goe [sic] to the Wilde Cust [sic]"*[2]. In 1658, Josua Nunez Netto and Joseph Pereira, Jews specializing in different Arawak dialects and serving as translators between the English and Dutch authorities and the native Indian tribes, arrived in Pomeroon, Guiana[3]. The native Indians had their own system for processing cocoa and the Jews learned it. Such innovative Jewish economic enterprises would become a hallmark of the people in their new home.

---

[1] Dr. H. Friedenwald, Material for the History of the Jews in the British West Indies, ib. No. 5, 1897

[2] Egerton Manuscript. British Museum , Volume 2395 , f. 46 . Cited by Oppenheim S. An Early Jewish Colony in Western Guiana, 1658 – 1666: and its Relation to the Jews in Surinam, Cayenne, and Tobago . Publications of the American Jewish Historical Society 1907 ; 17 : 95 – 186 .

[3] https://www.jewishvirtuallibrary.org/french-guiana-virtual-jewish-history-tour

In the earliest times, relations with Native Americans played a major role in the establishment of the displaced Jews who found their way to the Americas, and at times in how the Indians fared in their relations with their new neighbors. Jews and American Indians have today, and have long had, much in common, including modern concerns regarding religious rights, assimilation, and the challenge of maintaining our own national languages and cultures while being a part of American society, and this affinity isn't new; Jews came into close contact with Indians across a wide swath of American history, from the old southeast among the Cherokee, Creek and others in the colonial era 1700's, to the Midwest and on to the Pacific coast in the late 1800's, and even in Indian Territory of the early 1900's. In many cases the two blended[4].

Jewish businessman Julius Meyer traded with Indian tribes in what today is Nebraska and lived with the Sioux Indians for years and learned their language, as well as five other Native American dialects. He later became the official Indian interpreter for the US Congress[5]. Many Jewish traders developed relations with the Indians and learned Indian languages. Abraham Mordecai translated and advised the Creeks, Moses Baruch traded with the Umatilla Indians in Oregon and became an advisor and translator for that tribe, and in a later generation in Los Angeles, Wolf Kalisher became a supporter to Chief Manuel Olegario of the Temecula tribe[6].

---

[4] Eli Birnbaum, History of the Jewish People (pg 21)
[5] http://www.jmaw.org/meyer-omaha-jewish/
[6] http://www.jmaw.org/kalisher-jewish-los-angeles/

Solomon Bibo, whose father was a cantor, went even further. After settling in Santa Fe in 1869, he married an Indian woman from the local Acoma tribe and in 1885 he was appointed as "chief". Chief Bibo enacted many reforms including modern agricultural techniques and founding a school for children, the Bibo family having many descendants in New Mexico today among Jews, Hispanics, and Indians alike. The experiences of Abraham Mordecai, and his son Benjamin, we will see are truly illustrative of how many Jews on the frontier who in time were lost to the Jewish people but whose rediscovery through research and genealogical inquiry, can help us appreciate their struggles[7].

As a person of Jewish descent on my paternal side, and Muscogee Creek Indian descent on my maternal side, I can sympathize with the difficulties faced by Benjamin Mordecai; living in changing times and amid communities in struggle with one another his life was like our own, filled with contradictions, accommodations, and transitions. There would be in the early days several Jewish Indian Traders among the Creek and Cherokee Nations besides our Abraham Mordecai; Moses Nunes[8], was a Jewish backcountry and colonially licensed Indian trader and interpreter to the Creeks, who along with his brother Daniel spoke several Indian languages and who like Abraham Mordecai, went on to father children with his mixed race (and likely formerly enslaved) wife[9].

---

[7] https://www.ifcj.org/news/stand-for-israel/the-ballad-of-old-mordecai/

[8] "The Blurred Racial Lines of Famous Families", Frontline, Public Broadcast System. Bryan v. Walton, 33 Ga.Supp. 11, 1864 WL 1124 (Ga. 1864)

[9] According to historian Mario de Valdes y Cocom, Rose was "the quadroon slave (and daughter) of Moses Nunes, a Jewish back-country trader among the Creeks."per "The Blurred Racial Lines of Famous Families", Frontline, Public Broadcast System. Bryan v. Walton, 33 Ga.Supp. 11, 1864 WL 1124 (Ga. 1864), on the other hand, says: "What was Moses Nunez?

The lives of many of these men reflect the realities of the racial systems of their day, with several married to mixed race women, such as Mordecai, Nunes, and Wolf. An interesting source of Jewish life in the closing days of the Wild West comes from Flora Spiegelberg, a Jewess who kept a diary about life out on the range[10]. Flora and her husband Willie settled in Santa Fe, New Mexico where she founded a school for Jewish children.

Activist, educator, writer, and founder of the Committee for Jewish Women and the Temple Emanu-El Sisterhood, Flora Langerman Spiegelberg (1857–1943).

Probably a Portuguese (Jew), as his name imports, from a left-hand marriage with a mulatto by the name of Rose; that from this connection sprang James Nunez, Alexander Nunez, and Fannie Nunez, who afterwards intermarried with George Galphin...."

[10] https://jwa.org/encyclopedia/article/spiegelberg-flora-langerman

Willie became the town's first mayor in 1884. The following story from Spiegelberg's diary is one of the most inspiring:

"One day four stagecoach passengers arrived in Santa Fe. The station master spotted a band of Indians approaching the log cabin station and yelled for the passengers to get back into their stagecoach. The Americans complied, but the German passenger was nowhere to be found. Finally, looking behind the log cabin, the station master saw the German passenger praying softly in Hebrew, a black skull cap on his head, a prayer shawl about his neck, and a prayer book in his hand.

The station master yelled that danger was approaching. Noticing the impatience and excitement of the passengers, the Jewish traveler calmly said, 'Good friends, put your trust in God and He will bring you safely to your journey's end.' Miraculously...the Indians did not attack, and the stagecoach departed safely."

Jews and American Indians indeed have much in common, and the two groups' exchanges were numerous and diverse over the centuries, proving sometimes harmonious when Jews' and Natives people's economic and social interests were in alignment, even while at other times relations could be fraught, since Jews were still outsiders, and often were settlers. American Jews could exploit Indian cultural, social, and political issues as much as other American settlers, and a few did. Yet the shared experiences seem to be much more prevalent in shaping the relations between those Jews who ventured into native lands. The blending of the descendants of many of the men we examine into today's Indian communities attest to the impact each had on the other.

The experiences of the Jewish-Indian interactions are diverse, and through looking at some of the individual Jews who made a place for themselves, temporary or permanent, in Indian Country, we can learn a little more of the essence of each people. The face-to-face encounters between Jews & Native Americans in the 18th & 19th centuries defy easy interpretation yet offer insights to we their descendants as to the meaning of identity on the frontiers of cultures and nations, then and now. Jewish settler life on the American frontier was usually tough, and the various sorts of encounters they had with Native Americans, around business, warfare, and the emerging American culture of Manifest Destiny offer us a glimpse into a little-known part of our history (Koffman, 2019).

In a chapter entitled "Indians and Israel in the 21st Century", we see a modern reversal of the lives of many of the Jewish men from earlier chapters; Abraham Mordecai, Herman Bendell, Julius Meyer, Solomon Bibo, Wolf Kalisher, and Louis Wolf; instead of their long-ago frontier lives as Jews who came to live among the Indians, we meet hundreds of Peruvian Indians who have chosen to convert to Judaism and relocated to Israel. The B'nai Moshe "Children of Moses" as they call themselves, (also known as Inca Jews), are a small group of several hundred converts to Judaism originally from the city of Trujillo, Peru, to the north of the capital city Lima.

The community was founded in 1966 by a local man of Trujillo named Villanueva, who faced great exclusion and prejudice in his native city because of his decision to convert from the Catholic Church to Judaism. Villanueva had visited Spain for a time, learning from the local Sephardic community, and upon his return, taught around 500 former Catholics in Trujillo about Judaism, igniting a spark which would ultimately lead to their conversion to Judaism and joining the Jewish people. Most B'nai Moshe now live in the West Bank, mostly in Kfar Tapuach. The modern experiences of the B'nai Moshe stand in contrast to the centuries old stories of the lone Jewish peddlers who wandered the frontiers of our country and in time founded the great Jewish communities of America today, yet both stories are about that space where Jew and Indian met and the heritage we as (American) Jews hold.

(above) B'nai Moshe, the "Inca Jews" gather in shul on Shabbat.

What we learn about identity, race, and America by examining the intersection of "tribal" peoples such as Indians and Jews is a universal story with complexity and multilayered meanings. Yes, Jews' treatment of native people in the colonial expansion did displace and sometimes killed Native Americans, as well as their later efforts to help establish and defend rights for them, implies that the cherished immigrant histories of Jews coming to these North American shores must now be understood in the context into which all American ethnic immigration does, settler colonial expansion.

Yet in looking at the lives of some of the individual Jewish men who came to call Indian Country home we find that the shared "tribal" roots, the "peoplehood" from which Indian and Jew alike emerge does set them apart form others to some degree. Despite Native Americans not being the "Lost tribes" of Israel as many in the earlier times supposed, the deep and ancient tribal roots of both peoples, the confrontation with hostile social forces, and subsequent resistance to assimilation, the love of their peoplehood exhibited by Jews and Native Americans alike, these point to a shared spirit of deep spirituality and a moving testimonial of tenacious survival that we as Americans, of any color or creed, can learn from.

As a Jew, Native American, and Oklahoman, the unique vantage point I have on the many shared traits of both communities suggest to me the true meaning of those bedrock values that lie at the heart of the Jewish and Indian historic experiences.

Hopefully from this small volume we will learn a bit about the courageous people who came before us and ourselves be braver people in meeting our times challenges. In learning a bit about the cross-cultural exchange of Jews and Indians since contact we find the pattern of what tomorrow may well hold.

(above) Charles Strauss and his son in Arizona 1883

Kindred Peoples

In the experience of this author, I have found many Jewish communities, like many other communities in our country, are unaware of the more than 500 federally recognized Indian tribes that remain today in the US, as well as dozens of unrecognized tribes. Many Jews are *"surprised to learn that Native American people are still around,"* as co-founder of Indigenous Bridges Ateret Violet Shmuel stated in an interview recently, from the vantage point as head of an organization seeking to build ties between Indians and Jews.

The ignorance of the other is often mutual, as among many Native Americans, thanks to centuries of forcible missionization means Jews are seen in deeply religious, often Christian, terms. Ateret Violet Shmuel went on to say that *"in the mind of many, Israel was an extinct ancient relic that vanished in the time of Jesus"*. Many Indians *"didn't realize that Jews still exist"* too.

Nevertheless, the ties between Jews and Indians in North America go back to the days of Columbus. There is a shared "tribal peoplehood", an identity based on a shared historical, cultural, genetic, and religious source; Jews from the West *"don't often think of our people in terms of an indigenous nation,"* said Shmuel. Yet for an increasing number of Jews the last century of struggle over the land of Israel and the Jews around the world who support the Jewish state has led to an increasing awareness of the meaning of belonging and indigeneity.

"If we look at the UN's definition – a nation with an ethno-genesis within a specific land-space; which has a unique culture, language, spiritual framework, dress and set of traditions which predate colonial contact, and which they intend to pass down to future generations – we obviously fit that category."

True, many contemporary Jews likely don't think of their particular "tribe" as the victims of colonial oppression, but when Jewish history is viewed from a different perspective, it might be said the Jews, an alliance of 12 tribes that settled together in one territory that they considered made for them by the Almighty and which they regarded as sacred may in fact be very like Native American tribes experiences across the centuries; the countless repeated efforts at assimilation and destruction by others are something both Jew and Indian know well.

The indigenous rights movement has gained strength in recent years, and the meaning of indigeneity has become socially more nuanced, and not everyone would call Jews "indigenous people" yet using many of the common meanings of the word, the Jewish people are the indigenous people of the land of Judea, modern day Israel. Thousands of years of archaeological and historical evidence shows that Judaism and the beginnings of Jewish people, started there and through countless conquests and imperialistic actions by larger nations, ethnic Jews have been exiled from the ancestral homeland, subsequently settled in every corner of the world, even as many maintained their identity under difficult circumstances and continue to do so.

Such displacement is a foundational reality for many of the nearly 40 tribes of Oklahoma today, most of whom were removed to the state from hundreds even thousands of miles away in the 1800's. As any Jew over the past thousand years who has said "Next Year in Jerusalem!" knows, such an expression is a verbal gesture to a deep and long held link to the Jewish peoples ties to the land of Israel, no matter where previous generations wandered to.

Judaism is a land-based tribal religion, and despite whether some Jews recognize it or not, Jewish religious practice is land-based and agrarian in nature, its participants sharing a tribal history across a cyclical lunar calendar. As a member of both Native American and Jewish communities of the Tulsa area, I have experienced firsthand how my (maternal) Muscogee Creek people and (paternal) Jewish People share rituals of giving thanks for the food, land, knowledge, and other benefits from the Creator.

That which Jews do every Friday, ritually welcoming in the "Angels of Peace", receiving the "Sabbath Bride" so to keep and remember Shabbat, is very alike Indian customs of welcoming ancestors in ceremony and having spiritually established sacred times and practices. Even the common observer sees that the two peoples share much. One can see how theories debated since colonial times of ties between the two became so prevalent.

Legends of the Lost Tribes

In the 8th century BCE, the Assyrians dispersed the Kingdom of Israel. This long-ago event began the legend to the Lost Tribes of Israel, and the repatriation of these lost tribes in time emerged as an integral part of the Jewish as well as Christian messianic vision. For centuries there have been Lost Tribe theories offered about countless "discovered" peoples, including the Native Americans. Interestingly, a work by one of our own from the Jewish community was among the first books to posit the Native Americans are the Lost Tribe theory.

Written by a Dutch rabbi, scholar, and diplomat Manasseh ben Israel his book *The Hope of Israel* (1650), theorized that the discovery of the Native Americans, whom he asserted were a surviving remnant of the Assyrian exile, harkened the arrival of the messianic era. In 1651, Thomas Thorowgood published *Jewes in America, Or, Probabilities that those Indians are Judaical*.

The notion of Indians as the Lost Tribes was popular among the early Americans of note, including Cotton Mather (the influential English minister), Elias Boudinot (the New Jersey lawyer who was one of the leaders of the American Revolution), and the Quaker leader William Penn. The idea was given new life after James Adair, a 40-year veteran Indian trader (and an ancestor of thousands of Indians from several tribes of northeast Oklahoma today), who documented in excruciating detail the seemingly Jewish features of American Indian religion and societal customs in his *The History of the American Indians...Containing an Account of their Origin, Language, Manners, Religion and Civil Customs* in 1775.

In the colonial era it was a common theory among many that the Jews were the Lost Tribes, yet some saw the idea as unlikely, including Thomas Jefferson, who was skeptical. In a letter penned to John Adams about Adair's belief, he wrote, *"He adopts all the falsehoods which favor his theory."* The idea would eventually find its final demise with the advent of modern genetic which revealed there was nothing to support the theory. Epaphras Jones, an American Bible professor suggested the obviousness of Indians being the Lost Tribes in 1831, saying that those *"conversant with the European Jews and the Aborigines of America... will perceive a great likeness in color, features, hair, aptness to cunning, dispositions for roving, &s."*

Rather than any actual historic ties, the theory thrived due to a passionate if misguided affinity among some 17th and 18th century Americans with the chosen people of Scripture, whom they saw themselves as like, and to many, replacing as G-d's people. Such identification helped Christian settlers envision their seizure and colonizing of native lands in New England, and later the rest of the continent, as a reenactment of Israel's journey into the Promised Land. In a 1799 Thanksgiving Day sermon, Christian Minister Abiel Tabbot told his congregation in Massachusetts as much.

> *"It has often been remarked that the people of the United States come nearer to a parallel with Ancient Israel, than any other nation upon the globe. Hence, 'OUR AMERICAN ISRAEL,' is a term frequently used; and common consent allows it apt and proper."*

Yet Jews and Native American nations both have similar historical experiences which we have discussed already; displacement, oppression, assimilationist aggression, and missionization that reveal the good Reverend Tabbot and so many like him assumptions as fanciful on their part at best, colonial and genocidal at worst. Examining the lives of some of the individual Jews who came to live among, and often influenced, the Indians and tribal communities where they operated on a social and economic level, will reveal that even as these Jews impacted the Indians they were among, the experience of these Jews among them shaped indigenous lives as well.

In some cases, in time the two would merge, a legacy down to this very day in families like my own and hundreds of others. Indeed, thousands of persons of shared indigenous American/Jewish extraction are emerging, as increasing numbers of peoples of Latin American origin return to the Sephardic Jewish roots their converso ancestors were forced to abandon; Many of these returnees to the faith have a great amount of American Indian ancestry too. In the 21st century the synthesis continues as we see when we meet the Inca Jews of Israel. The relationship between Jews and Indians was hardly monolithic. Although there was oppression and exclusion, there was also cooperation, alliance, and cultural brokerage that occurred. These are the themes common in any frontier zone where cultures come into contact, collide, and connect. Sociology tells us that frontiers are geographic zones of interaction between two or more distinctive cultures, places where cultures contend with one another and with their physical environment to produce a dynamic that is unique to time and place (Horowitz, 1985).

The historian David Weber states that the frontier is the focal point of all history, the place where multiple cultures meet, clash, and exchange (Weber, 1982). Documents tell us of the past, yet these scant primary sources, limited, of course, by having been written by Europeans for their own purposes, can only go so far. That the American Indian perspective on their interactions with Jews is less known is for certain, but the documents we have do allow for glimpses of the complicated dynamics of Amerindian and Jewish interaction in the frontier past at least.

In the following pages we will look at several men who reveal the foreignness of their experiences in the 1700 and 1800's as Jews amid the rugged frontier, individuals who share a fate as those Jews who found relationships among Native Americans that would shape their lives, and that of their descendants in many cases. The rugged frontiers of our country's past are places where peoples who are "in between" such as the Jews and Amerindians inhabit ambiguous and shifting spaces where boundaries cross and change.

Such frontiers are where what is central and what is peripheral is often uncertain, and where the divisions between individual, groups, and states is porous. These frontiers, physical and cultural, were the clay we today were molded from, by the hand of Jew, Indian, and all who made their way in days gone by. We will start with Abraham Mordecai, a man who made a home among my mother's Creek people and who, with his first cotton gin, shaped the future of the entire American south, and the United States.

Abraham Mordecai

As a Creek person, and descendant of many who once called Alabama home, I first heard of Abraham Mordecai as one of the earliest white settlers of the area, a Jew, and an "Indian Countryman", as well as the man who brought the first cotton gin to the state, an event that changed the fate of many Alabamians of any color later. Abraham Mordecai (1755-1850) was among the earliest of non-Indian residents, and likely was the first Jew, to settle in what was then the Creek Nation and is now Alabama. He was an exceptional personality on the scene, as he played a part in many of the events that shaped the Southeast, including the American Revolution, the War of 1812, and the Creek War of 1813-14.

He was instrumental in the development of Alabama's early statehood efforts and its economic development as well. He had a long life, during which he was involved in many pursuits, engaging at times in being a negotiator (between the Indian tribal leaders and American federal and state governments), an Indian trader, a scout for the American military, as well as a founding developer from the beginning of the cotton industry around Montgomery (Messing, 1905).

Abraham Mordecai was born in Philadelphia, Pennsylvania, on October 24, 1755, to a family of Jewish merchants. A Jew by birth, he was related to the Cohen, Levy and Mordecai families of Norfolk and Charleston, though little is documented of his early life, and he was known to have served in the American Revolution as did many Jews in the colonial times, like my ancestor, Abraham Glymph.

Like Glymph, it appears that the colonial rugged frontier life led Mordecai to marry outside of his faith and live a unique life. The largest source of most published information concerning this extraordinary and enterprising Jew is from Colonel Albert James Pickett, the celebrated author of the *History of Alabama*. It appears that on the 30th of September 1847, the Colonel visited the aged Mordecai at his home in Dudleyville, in Tallapoosa County, Alabama.

Notes of the personal interview which followed between the elderly frontiersman and the celebrated historian are yet preserved in Pickett's own handwriting in the Department of Archives and History of the State of Alabama. We also have an (unpublished) book with information on the family by Mordecai's son Benjamin as well.

By 1783, Mordecai, describes by Pickett as a "queer fellow" " and as a "dark-eyed Jew", one said to be "of amorous disposition" towards Native American women, had settled among the Indians and established a trading business at Line Creek (in present-day Chambers County, Alabama) trading with the Creek town at Cusseta, near what is now Fort Benning on the Alabama-Georgia border (Messing, 1905). According to an original document on the family written by his son Benjamin White Cloud Mordecai, Abraham was married to a mixed-blood daughter of the famous Cherokee Chief Doublehead and his (likely) Afro-Indian wife Patsy[11]. Excerpted from the document written by Abraham's son Benjamin is information on the Mordecai family.

---

[11] While the number of Doublehead's children, records, and testimony of descendants suggests that Doublehead had as many as five wives, there are only two that are named in

"I was born in the Cherokee Nation, March 20th in 1800. My grandfather was a chief of the Cherokee Nation his name was Doublehead, my grandmother was a white woman her name was Patsy Doublehead. My father was a Dutch Jew, his name was Abram Moses Mordeceai, he came to the Nation in 1793, where he married my mother. They had nine children of which I was the oldest."

Though we know a lot about Abraham's life from the writings by Pickett in **History of Alabama**, the writings by his son Benjamin, who will look at in another chapter, is more personal and intimate data about the man. Mordecai, in true Jewish frontiersman style, served as a middleman for the Muscogee Creeks, trading pelts and other items for goods and utensils he acquired in Pensacola, Savannah, and other cities. He like so many other Jews of the frontier times would make his start as a peddler and build from there.

In his many trips into the wilds of Kentucky and Tennessee, he came upon white women and children who had been taken captive by the Shawnee and Chickasaw in the many frontier wars that raged as settlers crept deeper and deeper into Indian Country. Because of his good relationship with the chiefs, and since he knew the trails and villages deep in the Indian Country, he was appointed by Indian Agent James Seagrove to arrange for their return release, which he successfully did. Mordecai like many other Jews on the frontier would act as a middleman in many cases.

documents: 1) Nannie Drumgoole and 2) Kateeyah Wilson, both named in depositions filed regarding Doublehead's estate and Eastern Cherokee applications of descendants.

Being "other", he could likely identify with the natives, who he likely believed were themselves some type of long-lost kinsmen, as the Lost Tribes of Israel was a popular notion[12]. Mordecai living in the wilderness as he did, had little contact with other Jews, and in time he married a Cherokee woman, according to the manuscript by his sone and other documents and statements the daughter of Cherokee Chief Doublehead and his wife Patsy, who according to statements about having "the blood of Ham", was likely part African American as well as Cherokee, and though we do not know if as many others during this period he believed that Native Americans were descendants of one of the fabled Lost Tribes of Israel; it was a popular belief, and he may well have.

Sources indicate that he initially attempted to speak with the Creeks when he first began to trade in Hebrew, possibly believing that their Muskogee language was a dialect of his own ancestral Hebrew tongue. Known among the Indians as Mekkochee, or Little Chief, he was among the first traders among the Indians of the area and was familiar far and wide to the tribesmen. In 1785, Mordecai move to the Creek town of Holy Ground, located along the banks of the Alabama River, close to modern day Montgomery. The enterprising tradesman again established a lively business there, trading among the Creek and Choctaw who lived close by (Messing, 1905).

---

[12] Britannica, The Editors of Encyclopaedia. "Ten Lost Tribes of Israel". Encyclopedia Britannica, Invalid Date, https://www.britannica.com/topic/Ten-Lost-Tribes-of-Israel. Accessed 25 May 2021.

In the 1790s, the American government started the "plan of civilization"[13], ostensibly to get the Indians to abandon their traditional pursuits of hunting and gathering from the forests and take up farming and manufacturing. Of course, the federal officials' ulterior motives were to acquire their hunting lands of the Indians which stretched for hundreds of miles.

Benjamin Hawkins, the American governments Indian Agent, was the administrator of the plan of civilization, and he sought Mordecai's help in 1802, in setting up a cotton gin near the Cusseta and other Creek Indian settlements, in present-day Montgomery County. Mordecai, having built the first cotton gin in the territory near the junction of the Coosa and Tallapoosa Rivers, was well positioned for the Indians who brought him raw cotton in their canoes, to keep his enterprise in operation[14]. The gin was burned by Indians in 1806, but the cat was out of the bag as to the future and the impact cotton would have on the southland and America (Pickett, 1900).

In classic Jewish style, Mordecai negotiated a contract with the firm Lyons and Barnett, a firm owned by two Jewish families in Georgia, to establish the gin to process cotton, hopefully cultivated by the local Indians and, of course, brokered by Mordecai.

---

[13] The plan of civilization was a federal development program created in the 1790s to address the so-called "Indian problem," the much-debated question among American politicians about how to go about opening up American Indian lands to Euro-American settlement. The task of implementing the plan of civilization among the Creek Indians of present-day Alabama and Georgia went to federal Indian agent Benjamin Hawkins, who lived among the Creeks from 1796 until his death in 1816.

[14] 1805 Walter Burling from Mississippi smuggled seed of a very productive and excellent quality upland cotton (G. hir-sutum) from the Spanish ruler of Mexico. Reportedly, he hid the seed in Mexican dolls. The resulting crosses of this cotton with Creole Black and Georgia Green Seed spread throughout the southeastern U.S

Erected just below the confluence of the Coosa and Tallapoosa Rivers, the gin was stationed along a trading path that would one day become part of the route of the Federal Road, near a racetrack owned by Creek leader Charles Weatherford and the father of future Red Stick Creek leader William Weatherford. Mordecai among with the Indians and operated his gin and traded peacefully for the most part.

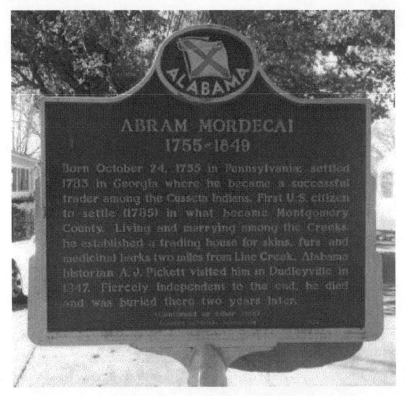

Historic Marker commemorating an Alabama Pioneer.

He was though, as noted later by Pickett, "of amorous disposition[15]" and one notable incident reflects that opinion. It was said that Mordecai made angry a local chief by offering too much attention to a married woman in his village, Mordecai losing an ear in the resulting fracas. He encountered more serious risks when he served with the Georgia Militia during the War of 1812, and on his return from that service to the country, he was immediately enmeshed in the Americans effort in the Creek War in 1813.

He served in that conflict as a scout, guiding military forces through the Creek Nation for Gen. John Floyd as they sought to engage the hostile Red Stick Creeks. Mordecai assisted the federal troops in locating Red Sticks who had been part of the attack on white settlers and allied Creeks at Fort Mims on August 30.

In November 1813, Mordecai led Floyd's unit as well as a force of allied Creek warriors under William McIntosh to the town of Autossee, engaging their enemies there, wherein the Red Sticks were routed, losing at least 200 men. Floyd's men and their Creek allies then fired the Indian town. Mordecai again guided Floyd's forces when they marched on Red Stick strongholds at Econochaca and other nearby villages the next year, but that time Floyd's men suffered a major defeat in a surprise Creek attack at Calabee Creek near Autossee (Messing, 1905).

---

[15] Excerpted from *"History of Alabama"*…"Towerculla (Capt. Isaak), chief of the Coosadas, hearing of his intrigue with a married squaw, approached his house with twelve warriors, knocked him down, thrashed him with poles until he lay in- sensible, cut off his ear, and left him to the care of his wife.. They also broke up his boat and burned down his gin-house. A pretty squaw was the cause of the destruction of the first cotton gin in Alabama."

Some researchers believe that Mordecai likely was present at the historic Battle of Horseshoe Bend, when the Red Sticks suffered their final defeat leading to the eventual removal of most of the Creek Nation to the Indian Territory west of the Mississippi, today's Oklahoma. Unknown to Mordecai at the time, in the years to come, his own family would be part of the infamous Indian Removal, as his wife and children moved to the Indian Territory while he would remain in Alabama.

After the conflict that including Horseshow Bend subsided, Mordecai set to work once again at his trading post, where he served as a cotton broker until 1836. This shameful episode of American history, when the Creek, Chickasaw, Choctaw, Seminole, and Cherokee Nations and other southeastern Indians were forcibly removed from their land by the federal government, would see Mordecai's family broken up since Mordecai remained behind in Alabama while his Cherokee wife and children removed west to the Indian Territory.

Mordechai who had spent much of his adult life among the Indians, probably sadly watched as she and her Indian people were forced to leave their native land, which was being swallowed by the state of Alabama, and were sent to the western "Indian Territory", what is now Oklahoma. He never learned if she reached Oklahoma safely or not sources say. After that, some observers report, his life lost a lot of its meaning for him and he lived in a small Indian hut, where he would one day build his own coffin according to Pickett, off which he ate his meals until he died at the age of almost 100 years (Pickett, 1900).

After the family's departure, finding himself at loose ends in an entirely new and white society than he had not been part of for many decades, Mordecai moved alone to Dudleyville, Tallapoosa County, Alabama and did what any good Jew would do…he established a store. The old Creek Nation he had known for so long was gone and he got busy adapting to a new life, alone, among white men[16].

Several years later, historian Albert Pickett conducted extensive interviews with Mordecai during his research for *History of Alabama: And Incidentally of Georgia and Mississippi from the Earliest Period*, and the well-known author also published an interview with Mordecai in Montgomery's Flag and Advertiser that same year. Many sources cite this work as the only source of information on Abraham but a recently surfaced autobiography by his son Benjamin has revealed a few known "facts" about Abraham to have been inaccurate, such as that his wife was a Cherokee, not a Creek though he was an Indian Trader among the Creeks.

During his final years, Mordecai lived simply in Dudleyville, passing away on August 25, 1850 and was buried in an unmarked grave in the Dudleyville Cemetery. On July 4, 1933, the Tohopeka Chapter of the Daughters of the American Revolution placed a granite marker on his grave in honor of his service during the American War of Independence[17].

---

[16] https://www.isjl.org/alabama-montgomery-encyclopedia.html
[17] https://alabamanewscenter.com/2019/10/24/on-this-day-in-alabama-history-abraham-mordecai-was-born/

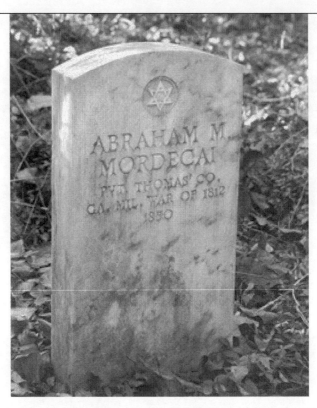

(above) the headstone of Abraham Mordecai, born in 1755. He was a veteran the American Revolution before settling in Georgia and establishing a trading business with the Creek Indians, trading furs, medicinal plants and other items for European goods acquired along the southeastern seaboard. He married a Cherokee woman and became known among that tribe as Mekkochee, or Little Chief.

Mordecai set up the first cotton gin in what is now Alabama and served in the War of 1812 and the Creek War in 1813. His wife and children left on the Trail of Tears without him, and he died alone in 1849.

Abraham Mordecai's Son Benjamin

Benjamin Moses Mordecai (aka Whitecloud)

Thanks to an unpublished book written by him and in possession of his descendants, we know that Benjamin Moses Mordecai was the son of Abraham Mordecai and his Cherokee wife, the daughter of Chief Doublehead, not a Creek woman as many sources assumed. We are fortunate that some of the original writings from his life have been preserved in this invaluable record by Benjamin's own hand and we can learn about him and his family in some detail, pictured below[18].

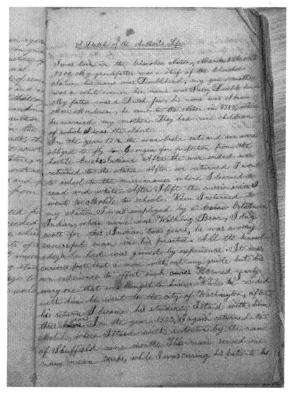

(above) a page of Benjamin Mordecai's hand-written manuscript

---

[18] http://benjaminmordecai.blogspot.com/

Also known as Chief White Cloud, Benjamin Mordecai certainly had an eventful life like his father did, living through times of great change and like his father transcending race and religion, overcoming educational and social barriers.

From what is gleaned from the few sources of information on the Mordecai family, especially the narratives from Pickett's writings, Abraham's wife Patsy was likely biracial Indian and black (according to wording Pickett used to describe Mordecai's wife, Patsy, "whose skin was "considerably darkened with the blood of Ham",) so her choosing to remain with the Indians rather than in Alabama after the removal history has shown to likely to have been a wise move for her and her children.

Patsy Mordecai was reported to be the daughter of Chief Double-head in her son Benjamin's manuscript; Doublehead is believed to have likely had several wives and consorts including possibly Nannie (Drumgoole) Doublehead (married about 1794 see Emmett Starr), Kateeyeah (Wilson) Doublehead (married abt 1797 estimated based on approx. ages of children), Creat Priber (daughter of Christian Priber), an unnamed Woman (Cherokee) Doublehead (married before 1768), and an unnamed Delaware Indian Woman (married before 1772), and finally Jennie Harrison (married before 1807)[19].

---

[19] While the number of Doublehead's children, records, and testimony of descendants suggests that Doublehead had as many as five wives, there are only two that are named in documents: 1) Nannie Drumgoole and 2) Kateeyah Wilson, both named in depositions filed regarding Doublehead's estate and Eastern Cherokee applications of descendants. Transcriptions at AMERIND-US-SE-L/200-12/0977343555 and AMERIND-US-SE-L/2000-12/0977343614 EC apps 10725(Bird Doublehead) 447

It was not uncommon for men, especially a chief to have children by enslaved women, this may be where Patsy comes from though the scanty records available give no indication of Patsy's mothers identity.

To white society Patsy would have been viewed as black but as the daughter of an influential chief such as Doublehead she would have found more security for herself and her children among the Indians, than among the white society of the time. So, she and Abraham Mordecai would separate after years together and several children born, he choosing to remain in Alabama and she traveling to a new home in the west again among her Cherokee people, who were rebuilding their lives in the west after the horrors of their displacement and Trail of Tears. His children in the west would have to fid their way in a Cherokee Nation of Indian Territory that was attempting to rebuild.

At the beginning of the 1830s, nearly 125,000 Indians lived on millions of acres of land in Georgia, Tennessee, Alabama, North Carolina and Florida, land their ancestors had occupied and cultivated for generations. By the end of the decade, very few natives remained anywhere in the southeastern United States. Working on behalf of white settlers who wanted to grow cotton on the Indians' land, the federal government forced them to leave their homelands and walk hundreds of miles to a specially designated "Indian territory" across the Mississippi River. This difficult and sometimes deadly journey is known as the Trail of Tears. The Mordecai family, minus Abraham, would resettle in the Cherokee lands west of the Mississippi.

Chief White Cloud
Ryan & Marker

Highland Presbyterian Mission

From what is known of their fate, as in any family, some descendants over the next several generations assimilated into mainstream "white" communities, such as what would occur with Benjamin's family, and others remained part of the Native American community in the Cherokee Nation in Indian Territory. Research on the fate of the several lines of descendants goes on, yet Abraham and Patsy's son Benjamin gives a good example of the intermixture of races, faiths, and destinies that typify all our varied ancestors' journeys as we became today's Americans, born from a complex melting pot.

Benjamin Mordecai's life exemplifies most the synthesis of the Jewish and Native relationships and their eventual amalgamation into an American heritage[20]. Research reveals that in his life, the meeting of Indian and Jew on a rugged frontier came to be consumed by the mainstream American, and in the case of Benjamin Mordecai, Christian experience.

His father was a Jew from Europe, his mother a mixed blood Cherokee, but "Benjamin White Cloud", as he appears in the Chicago City Directory in 1869, lived for some part in the native world as a younger man. Yet in time he came to moved away from his mother's Cherokee Nation and way of life, he preached the Christian gospel (exemplified by his "License To Preach", filed in February 9, 1859 in the tribal offices of the Cherokee Nation, Arkansas Territory) and eventually lost touch with his paternal Jewish roots, eventually ending his life journey in Chicago having preached the gospel for years.

---

[20] https://archive.org/details/PREFACE

In his active life Benjamin was a doctor and a preacher, and several primary documents, including his unpublished handwritten manuscript, exist that attest to his life and times. As Benjamin left Indian Territory for New York, he obtained letters from the places where he preached; above is his "License to Preach" Issued on February 9, 1859 by the "Cherokee Nation Arkansas Territory."

As will be discerned in his short biography recounted from the unpublished book he penned, his interest in medicine and curing led him to study under several Indian (Cherokee, Catawba), then white, doctors. The times he lived in were changing fast and he would in time pursue a life in the American mainstream, or as he puts it "living among the whites", and away from his Cherokee roots. As a lifelong resident of native communities, I observe that the terminology and usages of words he displays in his autobiographical sketch are ones that reveal a man still deeply shaped by his indigenous upbringing, even years after establishing a new life among non-Indians in Chicago.

A wonderful research effort by his descendants has revealed much primary source documents about him and his travels, and hopefully research will reveal more about the Mordecai family, and Benjamin in particular. His life was complex indeed. An excerpt from a blog post about him by a descendant reveals this multifaceted life of adapting to a world so different form that of his parents, yet he persisted.

"While we certainly don't have a complete picture of where Benjamin lived and when he lived there, we do have some clues from his written biography, historical documents, and the letters he received while preaching. This first map shows a possible progression of Benjamin from his possible birthplace in Alabama (where his father Abraham lived) to the Cherokee lands in Arkansas, to upper New York just south of Lake Ontario, to Dowagiac, Michigan where he obtained a medical license and he and his wife had their first 2 children, to Chicago where their son Benjamin was born, to Deerfield, IL where he died."

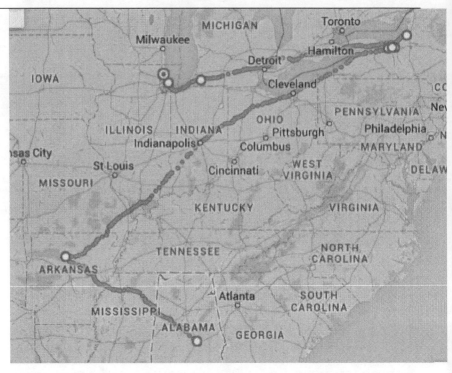

The travels of Benjamin "White Cloud" Mordecai during his life crossed geographical, cultural, racial, and religious lines.

"Benjamin is listed in the Chicago City Directory in 1869, a year before his death.

Name: Benjamin M Whitecloud

Residence Year: 1869

Street address: 99 Butterfield

Residence Place: Chicago, Illinois, USA

Occupation: Physician

Publication Title: Chicago, Illinois, City Directory, 1869"

The following is transcriptions from the unpublished book written by Benjamin Mordechai himself, and owned by one of his descendants, is a treasure trove of information on the man and family.

"I was born in the Cherokee Nation, March 20th in 1800. My grandfather was a chief of the Cherokee Nation his name was Double-head, my grandmother was a white woman her name was Patsy Doublehead. My father was a Dutch Jew, his name was Abram Moses Mordeceai, he came to the Nation in 1793, where he married my mother. They had nine children of which I was the oldest.

In the year of 1812 the war broke out and we were obliged to fly to Georgia for protection from the hostile Creek Indians. After the war ended, we returned to the Nation. After we returned, I went to school to the missionaries where I learned to read and write. After I left the missionaries I went to Mobile to school. When I returned to the Nation I was employed by a Catawba Indian, whose name was Walking Bear. I dug roots for this Indian two years, he was a very successful man in his practice. All the knowledge he had was gained by experience.

It was a curious fact that a man without any guide but his own experience to effect such cures. He cured nearly every one that was brought to him. While I resided with him, he went to the city of Washington after his return I became his student, I staid with him three years.

In the year 1823, I again returned to Mobile, where I staid with a doctor by the name of Shuffield nine months. This man served me many mean tricks, while I was curing his patients, he was pocketing the money. I advise all patients to beware of a Yankee. After being duped by this Yankee, I returned to my own Nation.

After this I studied under a Cherokee Indian Doctor for two years, when he was murdered by the white men, this man was very kind and skillful, I hardly thought before this time that the whites were capable of such barbarities.

After the death of my old friend I again returned to Georgia and commenced practicing. I did not use any mercurial preparations in my practice and the consequence was I met with opposition on every hand from the old school or calomel doctors. I advise all to beware of mercurial and mineral medicines. These poisons, instead of removing the disorder, for to relief of which they are administered, only tend to confirm the disease more strongly, dooming the victim to slow but certain death.

The great God of heaven, in his vegetable kingdom, has provided remedies for the treatment of all manner of diseases, to which the frail constitution of man is subject.

I speak this not from my own alone, but from the experiences of hundreds of others who have been snatched, as it were, from the grave by the use of vegetable medicines. But I have regressed from my subject.

After staying in Georgia about one year, I then returned to Mobile where I found a medicine college had been organized during my absence, there physicians were followers of the celebrate Doctor Thomson. I immediately took a course of lectures which lasted nine months.

It may not be amiss to state, that I was very much respected by all classes of community because I was a red man. I shall always be under obligation to Doctors Everett and Clark who took a great deal of trouble to instruct me, both in language and physic.

The Indians who came to this college for instruction were allowed to hear the lectures and verbal instruction free of charge. After finishing my course of lectures at this college, I went to the Creek Nation, where I practiced under a Creek doctor for six months, here I learned a great deal of valuable and interesting knowledge. Ever since that time I have lived among the whites.

I have cured many of all kinds of diseases, and I hope, by the grace of God, to cure many more, the remedies mentioned in the following work, are not conclusions drawn merely from theory, but the result of successful practice of many years. The more a person studies the products of the vegetable kingdom, the more he finds remaining to be learned."

- Benjamin Moses Mordeceai

<><><>

Benjamin's death record has not been found, but he is listed in the 1870 Census for Deerfield in the deceased section. He would never return to his Cherokee Nation roots. His wife Mary and his three kids - Abraham, Hattie & Benjamin - are also recorded as living in Deerfield, Illinois in 1870.

(Above) heirloom ceremonial items of Benjamin Mordecai kept in the family by his descendants to this day.

Today many generations later, the inheritors of Abraham Mordecai's legacy are scattered among most of the races, religions, and ways of life in America, his descendants counting in the tens of thousands, many unaware of his fascinating life or role in history. Family reunions have been held and research into the interesting family is continuing[21].

---

[21] http://benjaminmordecai.blogspot.com/

The experiences of Abraham and his son Benjamin are truly illustrative of how many Jews on the frontier, who in time were lost to the Jewish people but whose rediscovery through research and genealogical inquiry can help us appreciate their struggles as Jewish people in a time of change, matter in the larger story. It also reveals the importance of community and the communal strength Jews find in one another; isolated and alone on the frontier, many of the Jews who eventually established families and businesses would weather the storms to come, even while others would in generation to come become lost to their descendants.

As a person of Jewish descent on my paternal side, and Muscogee Creek Indian descent on my maternal side, I can sympathize with the difficulties faced by Benjamin Mordecai; living in changing times and amid communities in struggle with one another and others. We can be sure his life was like our own, filled with contradictions, accommodations, and transitions. While Benjamin's predilection to preach the Christian gospel in his own time despite his father's Jewish identity reveal just one example of the unraveling of the Jewish legacy in one family on the frontier.

Nonetheless the life of Benjamin like that of his father Abraham was on of enterprise and innovation, truly Jewish in that aspect. Jews and their descendants would transform with the times like all people do, some away from their Jewish roots, and others closer to them.

Moses Nunes

Like Abraham Mordecai after him, Moses Nunes was also a Jewish colonial era trader among the Indians of the southeast, arriving early at the founding of the Georgia colony and in time playing an important role in the colonial southeast, as did many of Jews. Historian Ralph Melnick has written that *"nearly everything one concludes from a study of Southern Jewry has its opposite that is equally true ... Nearly everywhere and in nearly everything some Jew has played a part. But it has been a marginal role."* The Jewish experience in Georgia has been no exception to this pattern.

The Nunes family, headed by Samuel Nunes, M.D., a Sephardi Jew, would arrive in colonial Georgia among the first settlers, establishing their new home there in Savannah in July of 1733. Savannah's recorded history begins in that same year, the year General James Oglethorpe and the 120 passengers of the good ship "Anne" landed on a bluff high along the Savannah River in February. Oglethorpe named the 13th and final American colony "Georgia" after England's King George II. Savannah became its first city.

The plan was to offer a new start for England's working poor and to strengthen the colonies by increasing trade. The colony of Georgia was also chartered as a buffer zone for South Carolina, protecting it from the advance of the Spanish in Florida. Under the original charter, individuals were free to worship as they pleased and rum, lawyers and slavery were forbidden at least for a time.

Upon settling, Oglethorpe became friends with the local Yama-craw Indian chief, Tomochichi.

The founding of Savanah in 1732 (from Landing at Savannah in Scribner's **Popular History of the United States**, *Volume III by William Bryant, 1897.)*

Oglethorpe and Tomochichi pledged mutual goodwill and the Yamacraw chief granted the new arrivals permission to settle Savannah on the bluff. As a result, the town flourished without warfare and accompanying hardship that burdened many of America's early colonies. So fledgling Savannah received its first Jews, not that it really wanted them. These new Jewish arrivals to Savannah had been unwanted at home in London and were not much more welcome in Georgia, but in the eyes of the Christian settlers, at least they were not Roman Catholics. Although religious toleration was beginning to emerge as a value during the Enlightenment, it was the pragmatic need to attract settlers that led to broad religious freedoms that drew the Jews to Savannah.

South Carolina wanted German Lutherans, Scottish Presbyterians, Moravians, French Huguenots, and Jews as a counter to the French and Spanish Catholic absolutist presence to the south, which Georgian settlers saw as a threat to the freedoms they had traditionally held (Bonomi, 1986). The Jews were useful in their capacity as non-Catholics at least.

On 6 April 1733 William Cox, the Georgia colonies' only physician died. In early July, a febrile illness struck the new colony taking the lives of three people in the early part of July. Among the timely new arrivals in Savannah was the Portuguese Jewish physician, Samuel Nunes. Eleven more of the English colonists died in July.

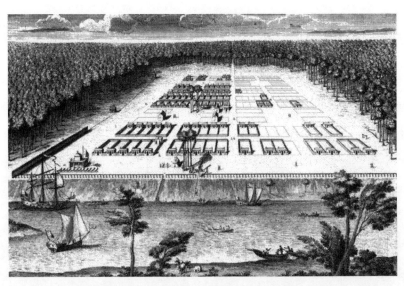

A View of Savannah by Peter Gordon, partially labeled to show layout of numbered lots. About 1734

But Oglethorpe credited Dr. Nunes with alleviating the epidemic and saving the colony[22]: 'He proceeded by cold Baths, cooling Drinks and other cooling Applications. Since which the Sick have wonderfully recovered.' While initially being reluctant to allow the Jewish settlers to join the colony, the actions of Nunes caused Oglethorpe to allow them to join the new colony.

The Nunes family did not arrive alone; Congregation Mickve Israel was founded by a group of 42 Jews who arrived together in Savannah, in the new colony of Georgia in 1733. Having left London, England, five months earlier, the brave band of mostly Portuguese Sephardi Jews and two German Jewish families sought freedom and opportunity in the New World.

Doubtless the trip on the William and Sarah was rough, and they ran aground near North Carolina. The first communal act upon landing in Savannah was the initiation of religious services. Worship was facilitated by the fact that more than a Minyan, the requirement of ten Jews present was immediately available, and a Torah Scroll was carried by the Jewish settlers to their new home in Georgia.

These founding families of Mickve Israel brought with them a "Safertoro" [sic] made of deerskin, with two "cloaks," and a "circumcision box," which was donated by a London merchant. This same Torah is still used on commemorative occasions at Mickve Israel to this day.

---

[22] Oglethorpe J. Letter to the Trustees [of Georgia colony] about December, 1733. John Percival, the Earl of Egmont Papers (Phillips Collection), See http://djvued.libs.uga.edu/egmont/epmenu.html , pp. 126–126

(above) Mickve Israel Synagogue in Savanah Georgia is America's third-oldest Jewish congregation, and the oldest Jewish congregation in the South. In 1820, the congregation built their first synagogue in Georgia at the corner of Liberty and Whitaker Streets. The small wooden structure was the first synagogue built in Georgia but in 1829 the temple was destroyed by fire.

On the same site a new brick building was built and consecrated in 1841. With the growth in Savannah's Jewish population, the congregation outgrew its structure. It planned for a new building and construction began in 1876 laying the cornerstone for its current structure on March 1, 1876. The completed building was consecrated two years later.

All but eight of the original forty-two Jewish colonists were Jews originally from Iberia who had arrived in London ten years earlier, most having lived as Crypto-Jews, publicly practicing Roman Catholicism, and secretly preserving their Jewish heritage, prior to their departure from Portugal and Spain. Among these Sephardim was Dr. Samuel Nunes Ribiero, a physician who had been imprisoned during the Inquisition for his successful efforts to convert New Christians back to the Jewish faith.

Of the eight Ashkenazi founders of the early Savannah congregation were the families of Abraham Minis and Benjamin Sheftall, whose descendants are benefactors and active participants in the congregation to this very day. In the Nunes family were Abigail, Daniel, Isaac, Moses, Rachel, and Rebecca. They would have had the same difficult time living in the new world as other settlers.

Though given land, in the form of town lots in the original square of Savannah, there was still a shortage of food and all other necessities. They arrived during the rough start of Georgia, just five months after General James Edward Oglethorpe established the colony.

Some of the family fled the town in 1740 when the Spanish in Florida threatened to invade and take possession of the new settlement. The thought of being under the heel of the nation which still enforced the dicta of the dreaded Inquisition were too much and several family members fled to Charles Town, more out of reach, and a bit more civilized.

But young Moses must have viewed the new country with eager eyes, and he was soon on the list of licensed Indian traders to the Creeks, overseeing the prestigious and prosperous store at Tukabatchi. Traditionally this was one of the most important Creek towns. Later, in the eighteenth century, its links to the Shawnee became a matter of constant agitation.

The mother of Tecumseh, great rebel leader of the Shawnees, as well as the mysterious Prophet, was from Tukabatchi and returned there to live after the death of her warrior husband. Moses Nunes is listed among the official Creek Traders with his partner Joseph Wright in 1750. In 1753 one notorious case in which Nunes was involved as a certified witness was when the powerful Creek Head Warrior Acorn Whistler led the ambush/murder of a group of Cherokee diplomats outside Charleston and the British demanded his death in exchange.

In a secret meeting the over-chiefs appointed the Whistler's young nephew to assassinate him in the woods, making the death a clan matter to avoid a wide war. Then they ordered that the young nephew be assassinated too, so they could not be blamed. Word of this leaked out and Nunes was one of those called on to solve the conspiracy. The affidavit and details of this case appear in *The Colonial Records of South Carolina, Documents Relating to Indian Affairs, 1750-1754*.

In the Records of 1754-1765 Capt. Daniel Pepper reports from Ockchoys of the Upper Creeks, 30th November 1756 that he signed a certificate in favor of Moses Nunes and Joseph Wright for the delivery of thirty-one horse loads of presents in the Creek Nation for which he agreed with Mr. Nunes to pay twenty pounds per horse load.

This was to be presented to the Creeks to keep them from joining the French side in the French and Indian War. Another entry from 1757 states that several Traders brought Negro Slaves illegally into the Creek Nation, one of these being Moses Nunes, who brought in one Negro. It is not stated whether this slave was male or female. George Galphin is not on this list of violators.

The role that Nunes played, like other Indian traders, was one of the intermediaries in matters such as those relating to the Acorn Whistler Affair and other situations that required a nuanced approach and knowledge of the Indians. Like other "Indian Countrymen" as the Indian Traders who lived and worked among the Indians were known, Nunes would father children with women not of the Jewish community.

A man of wealth and distinction and a member of Oglethorpe's Masonic Lodge, he was successful by the standard of the times. Moses served successfully as an Indian interpreter and an agent for the Georgia Revolutionary forces[23]. As the decades passed the frontier was changing, and he would have lineages that scattered through several different communities.

---

[23] Detail Moses Nunez 5 Nov 1763 https://www.newspapers.com/clip/54244533/moses-nunez/?xid=637

In his will of October 14, 1785, Moses divided his property equally among his children born to his first wife Rebecca Abraham (who born a son Samuel) and to his second wife Mulatto Rose (born sons James, Robert and Alexander and daughter Frances Galphin). On page 264 of Hawkins Letters in a letter from John Randon to Hawkins involving queries about property in Randon's father's estate about land and slaves, he writes "*Some of the lands were left in the hands of old Nunns (Nunes), father of half-breed Samson, for 400 and the other 180 pounds sterling.*"

Rose was an enslaved "Mulatto" who belonged to Moses Nunes, his trade among the Creeks offering many such situations he surely took advantage of. It is possible that she is the "Negroe Slave" Nunes transported illegally into Tukabatchi in 1757 and was fined as listed in the S.C. Indian Commission records. This date would be about right for the time Rose was present there. She was born about 1744, so at that time she would have been about twelve years old.

Data from the will of Moses Nunes, written 14 October 1785 identifies a Mulatto Rose, whom he firmly calls his wife, and mother of his four children, Samuel, James, Robert, and daughter Frances Galphin (wife of George Galphin II). (Possibly she is the same Mulatto Rose who bore George I. Galphin's daughter, Barbara Galphin.)

The copy of the will comes from The Jacob Rader Marcus Center of the American Jewish Archives, Cincinnati, Ohio, accessed with the help of Archival Resident, Christine A. Crandall.

The handwritten will of two pages is signed by Moses Nunes in a firm hand and witnessed by David Montaigut and Joseph Abraham. He names two sons, Samuel and James, and George Galphin (II) as his executors. The existence of the will is confirmed in "***Georgia Intestate Records***", page 236. Rose is always referred to as "Mulatto Rose" by Nunes in his will.

He does *"order and confirm and I do give unto the above-mentioned Mulatto Rose and her three sons James, Robert and Alexander Nunes, and her daughter Frances Galphin* (wife of George II Galphin) *being all my issue, a full and perfect freedom from all slavery and servitude, in reward and as an acknowledgment of the faithful conduct and behaviour of the said Mulatto Rose toward me and my children."*

He acknowledges that his oldest son Samuel is also her son and his. Possibly he had already freed Samuel before the will was written. The meaning of the word "Mulatto" in the document and its usage there is debatable; It once meant a person of mixed blood, and could mean someone of Indian and white, or black and white, or all three. Recently it has meant half white and half black in some groups. It has been implied that she was what came to be called a quadroon, that is of one quarter African blood. It is not known whether she was ever actually the property of George I Galphin.

In his will, he claims that she is deceased. This may have been for daughter Barbara's sake. One source, as researched and written by Mario de Valdes y Cocom, in his PBS Tri-Racial research, believed that the Slave Rose who bore Barbara was a quadroon daughter of Moses Nunes.

Likely the relationships of Galphin's and Nunes' children were tangled; In the 1830 Census Index of Georgia, there are four Nunes entries: Charles Nunes colored 1830 Burke County; Janet Nunes (colored) 1830 Burke County; Joseph Nunes (colored) 1830 Burke County; Robert Nunes (colored) 1830 Burke County.

A note says "Eunier same as Nunes" Daniel Eunier (colored) 1830 Appling County Hugh Eunier (colored) 1830 Appling County. According to a posting of one descendants' story, Nunes descendants lived among the Creeks.

"This daughter of Mulatto Rose and Moses Nunes probably met young George II at Tuckabatchee where she may have lived as a girl with her father and mother. She and her brothers might have lived an Indian life. Nunes had at least one Creek wife, so there were half Creek Nunes children too. There is no word of Frances and George II having children. If they did, these children might have been raised in Tuckabatchee or Coweta as Creek children.

They might have been cared for by Metawney. Frances probably travelled around with her husband, and they might have had houses in both Washington County at the new Galphinton Trading Post and at some site in Burke County across from Silver Bluff. Because she was a half-sister of Barbara Galphin Holmes, she probably visited with that family. Barbara had several acreages in Georgia and would certainly have allowed her half-brother George II and her maternal half-sister Frances to use these places in which to live.

In *The National Genealogical Society Quarterly*, vols. 1-85, page 300, list of freed slaves living in Georgia: Nunes, no first name age 23, born in South Carolina, brought into GA. while an infant. Nunes, Alexander age 40, born in Savannah, Ga.; Gaulphin, Frances age 43, born in Savannah, Ga.; Nunes, Rose age 75, born in Savannah, Ga.; Nunes, Robert age 16, born in Burke County, Ga.; Nunes, Genett age 17, born in Burke County, Ga.[24]"

The historic data available reveals that the descendants of Nunes would come under the increasingly racially exclusive laws of Georgia as the colony developed over time, and while some families who came to colonial Georgia on board the William and Mary in 1733 would go on to be recorded as leading Jewish families in the Georgia, Carolina, and other colonies for generations to come, such as Sheftall and Minis, other families descendants would intermarry among the Indians and African American community, disappearing into the mix of the early American society, such as some descendants of the Nunes family.

---

[24] Per the family of Joseph Alston and Caroline Green Hatcher, 2013-05-05.

(above) The 'Old Jewish Burial Ground' in Savannah. The City of Savannah has two Old Jewish Burial Grounds, initially established as a gesture of goodwill by James Oglethorpe shortly after the Jewish immigrants' arrival to Savannah in 1733. Oglethorpe set aside a plot of land to be used as their burial grounds. The second came to the Jewish citizens by way of King George III. In 1762, Mordecai Sheftall, the son of Benjamin Sheftall, one of the original passengers on the William and Sarah, asked King George III to grant him land to create a cemetery. A parcel was granted that "shall be, and forever remain, to and for the use and purpose of a Place of Burial for all persons whatever professing the Jewish Religion." In 1773, Mordecai Sheftall founded The Jewish Community Cemetery just outside the city walls.

Herman Bendell

A newly appointed Jewish Superintendent of Indian Affairs attempting to convert Indians to Judaism was the fear of many at the time who fought his appointment, though such fears proved unfounded as Dr. Herman Bendell, a physician from New York that President Ulysses Grant appointed to direct the Arizona Territory's Indian Affairs took his post amid criticism. The Boston Pilot newspaper worried that Dr. Bendell would "undo" the conversion work of Christian missionaries, spreading Judaism to the tribal peoples of Arizona where he was posted. This did not happen, of course.

(above) Herman Bendell as a young soldier in the Union Army during the Civil War, serving with both the 6th New York Heavy Artillery and the 86th New York Infantry. Dr. Bendell served with the Army of the Potomac, the Sheridan Campaign, and in the Shenandoah Valley.

Dr. Bendell and his lifestyle as an observant Jew was among several reasons that President Grant posted him to the position since he sought an Indian Commissioner who would make the welfare of the Indian a goal over Christian missionization as was the status quo.

(above) Indian Commissioner Dr. Herman Bendell, 1871

Dr. Bendell turned out to be a fair and conscientious man and Indian Commissioner, though not without much criticism and unsubstantiated allegations directed his way during his tenure.

"I feel it is a duty I owe to the people of the Country and the Indians under my charge to do something to relieve the pressures that surround them."

For two years he did the job the president appointed him to despite great opposition and challenging circumstances, mainly due to his Jewish identity. His appointment was a heavy responsibility, coming as it did at a difficult period for the Arizona Territory whose government sought to remove the many tribal groups which were long nomadic to reservations, hoping to settle them into a lifestyle of sedentary farming, despite the environmental and culture challenges to such as scheme.

Dr. Bendell's reporting to Indian Affairs commissioner Francis Amasa Walker, was reprinted in New York Times, pointing out the resistance by most of the Indians to cooperate with resettlement on the reservations, where conditions offered by the Government were meager at best.

Dr. Bendell sought a larger budget for the plan to settle, as the original amount set aside was for three Chiricahua reservations, and by 1872 there were seven, which meant more resources for the Indians now necessarily settled on reservations with little resources excepting a government dole. Despite these small victories, Dr. Bendell would find little appreciation for his efforts (Schwarz, 1979). Nevertheless, he met antisemitism with grace. Though the Board of Indian Commissioners praised Dr. Bendell's accomplishments, they still recommended he be replaced by a Christian.

> *"Dr. Herman Bendell, Superintendent of Indian Affairs for Arizona, is a most excellent official, a man of splendid judgment, strict integrity, who has managed the affairs of the office to entire satisfaction, but unfortunately he is not a Christian."*

After a short stint as Consul to Denmark (President Grant's conso-lation appointment) and a year studying ophthalmology at Heidelberg, Bendell and his family settled down to a rewarding life in Albany, New York where he enjoyed a prominent medical practice and engaged civic role in the community for the rest of his life. On September 16, 1873 Dr. Bendell married Wilhelmine Lewi, the daughter of Dr. Joseph Lewi, in a ceremony performed by the reform Rabbi Isaac Mayer Wise[25]. Herman Bendell died on November 14, 1932 in Albany, NY, at the age of 89, with few of those who knew him back east realizing that Dr. Bendell, longtime New York state ophthalmologist, had once strived to secure Indian rights in pre-state Arizona[26].

Dr. Bendell was a part of the history of American Jewish relation-ships with Native Americans, as it is in the realm of modern people's imagination and in the realities of the face-to-face encounters. These two groups' exchanges were numerous and diverse, proving at times harmonious when Jews' and Natives people's economic and social in-terests aligned, but discordant and fraught at other times. Dr. Bendell is an example of the many times Jews on the frontier helped Indian people navigate their dealings with the American society, as Jews were doing as well. Julius Meyer who we will look at next, like Dr.Bendell, played a much larger and more intimate role in the fate of the lives of Indians he knew

---

[25] "Married". Daily Albany Argus. Albany, New York, United States of America. Sep 19, 1873. p. 1.
[26] "Obituary, Dr. Herman Bendell". Star-Gazette. Elmira, New York, United States of America. Nov 15, 1932. p. 39.

Julius Meyer

Julius Meyer was among the earliest of Jews to arrive in the Nebraska Territory, coming when it was till the Wild West and the Indian tribes still dominated the prairies. Born in Bromberg, Prussia, March 30, 1839, he emigrated to Omaha in 1866, just a year before Omaha was incorporated as a city and Nebraska was admitted to the Union as a State. He joined his older brothers Max, Moritz and Adolph who had established a cigar store and a jewelry/music store.

Meyer created his own niche in the rough and tumble of the frontier, trading goods from his siblings' stores with the local tribes like the Ponca, many of whom who would be removed to the Indian Territory todays Oklahoma. Traveling by horse through the wildlands of the Indian-controlled areas, he would live for weeks with tribal peoples in their remote communities conducting trade.

Nebraska was organized as a territory in 1854, and within a year the stream of Jewish settlement had begun. The first Jewish settlers are believed to have been two brothers, Lewis and Henry Wessel, who went to Nebraska City from St. Louis in 1855. The next few decades brought a steady trickle of Jews who were predominantly of Central European origin (Alsace-Lorraine, Germany, Bohemia)

. Many had settled briefly in cities on the eastern seaboard before moving to the west, where, especially after the Civil War, the Homestead Act and railroad construction attracted new settlement. The early Jews in Nebraska were mainly merchants.

A Stereoview showing Meyer with an unidentified man, woman, and child, possibly Poncas.

Meyer would learn to speak several Indian languages, something which distinguished him from many traders of the time. As well setting him apart from other, often unsavory White men the Indian were dealing with, he treated Native people fairly. Despite living with Indians in the backcountry for weeks at a time, Meyers was also known to have been very observant of the laws of Kashrut, adhering to the Jewish dietary laws even in such difficult circumstances as his was when in Indian Country.

When Meyer took part in ceremonial feasts with tribal leaders, it is said the Indians knew to serve him hard boiled eggs instead of the non-kosher meats other participants ate. In Omaha, Meyer established an "Indian Wigwam" store that did well selling native crafted items. He served as an interpreter for Gen. George Crook.

The Omaha Daily Bee reported on March 18, 1900: *"Of all the stories told by Julius Meyer relative to his long experience with the Indians away back in the early history of Nebraska, none are more interesting than his recital of a tour he once made with Hermann, the celebrated magician [of the renowned Hermann family of performers in magic]."* Meyer said that Hermann, while visiting Omaha during the 1870s, had "expressed a desire to see the Indians in their natural state." Accordingly, Meyer and Hermann *"set forth for the country occupied by the Sioux tribes. He was anxious to mystify the Indians with his tricks, and soon after our arrival he was given an opportunity."*

After Meyer had convened a group of curious Sioux, *"[t]he magician performed several clever tricks, which greatly pleased and astonished the Indians. . . . At last Hermann asked to borrow a hat. An Indian named Fighting Horse was the first to respond. . . . Holding the hat in his hand, Hermann made a little speech, the substance of which was that while he usually received pay for his entertainments, he was not on that occasion asking anything. Then he scanned the hat closely for a moment and nodded that he had found enough money in it to compensate him most liberally for his work. . . . [and] drew out a roll of bills aggregating $600."*

What happened next surprised both Meyer and Hermann. "'That's my money; It was found in my hat,' roared Fighting Horse. For once the man whose business it was to puzzle other people was himself puzzled. He couldn't afford to give that Indian so much money," and a lengthy conversation followed. Fighting Horse, supported by the other Indians, continued to insist loudly that the money belonged to him because it had been found in his hat.

At last, the leader Spotted Tail, was appealed to-but he supported Fighting Horse. When Meyer tried to explain that finding the money had been one of Hermann's tricks, "Spotted Tail replied: 'A man who can perform a trick once can do the same trick again. Let him give Fighting Horse that money and then reach in the hat again and get more for himself. Then they will both have money. That's fair.'" Meyer replied that "Hermann was not prepared to repeat the trick just then, but that he might do so if given a little while in which to rest.

This was to give Hermann an opportunity to get away. But the Indians would not accept such a proposition. They wanted Hermann to remain in sight. He stood upon an improvised platform and there they wanted him to remain until the question was settled." In desperation Meyer "finally suggested that the only way Hermann could perform the trick over again would be to have another hat just like that of Fighting Horse, and that the same hat could not be used twice. I knew there was no such hat in the crowd. But not to be outdone, the Indians said they knew a man a few miles away who had a hat like the one Hermann had used.

A messenger was dispatched for the hat. "While he was gone Hermann was given time to arrange for a repetition of the trick. When the hat was produced the Indians examined it to see that it had no money in it. It was then passed over to Hermann and he drew from it the same roll of bills that he had apparently found in Fighting Horse's hat. Then they believed it was really a trick, and Hermann could keep the money." Julius Meyer was known among Indians as Box-ka-re-sha hash-ta-ka and was made their official interpreter.

He was a friend of the Indians, and he was highly trusted by chiefs Spotted Tail, Red Cloud, Sitting Bull, and Swift Bear. Meyer closed the Indian Wigwam store in 1880 but retained his close association with the Indians. In 1883, he was hired by French government to accompany a group of Indians to Paris. Julius Meyer remained an admirer of the arts despite his wild west life and was a founder of the Omaha Symphony and with his brother Max was a cofounder of Nebraska's first synagogue, known today as Temple Israel.

The historic records reveal that Meyer was one of the most interesting Jews in the annals of the settling of the west. His involvement in crucial events that continue to shape modern Indian life today make the role he played in many agreements between Indians and the federal government important. As well his work later in life with his community of faith and the arts reveal him to be an amazing man who was a true trailblazer.

Julius Meyer in front of his store at 163 Farnam Street, Omaha, Nebraska, about 1875, with chiefs who he translated for. In the late 1860s when he opened his Indian Curiosity shop, called the "Indian Wigwam Emporium" in Omaha, it was a unique enterprise for the times. Julius Meyer was born in Prussia in 1839 and emigrated to Omaha, Nebraska in 1867. He started developing relationships with the Plains Indians and was purportedly able to speak six different Indian languages. He served under General George Crook as an interpreter.

Photograph of Indian Interpreter Julius Meyer with Sioux Chiefs, circa 1870s; The subjects are identified on the obverse, "Julius Meyer Interpreter, & Indian Chiefs. Spotted Tail, Iron Bull, and Pawnee Killer". The reverse: "Indian Wigwam 234 Farnam Street, Omaha, Neb. Julius Meyer, Box-ka-re-sha-hash-ta-ka. Indian Interpreter. Indian trader and dealer... Tomahawks, Bows & Arrows, Covers, Pipes, Scalps, Moccasins, Garments, Beadwork..."

(above) Julius Meyer served as trusted interpreter for the Indians throughout the years of his work. Meyer with Pawnees, identified as Te-Taska-ke-rook; Ta-la-ka; La-tack-kach-ta-ka; Julius Meyer; Tau-e-gut-le-sha; Le-stachke-ge-re; La-ga-lash-line; Tou-rahe-sha-kish[27]

[27](https://nebraskahistory.pastperfectonline.com/photo/3E57ABF8-2BAE-449D-B9D3-793839638569)

As one commenter on his life said "I was amazed: a boy-chik from Europe who some-how gained the confidence of a group of people rightly suspicious of the white man? An Israelite adventurer who once conversed with the free-living masters of the mountains and plains?"; Like dozens of young Jewish entrepreneurs who migrated to the burgeoning towns and cities, farms and homesteads, near Indian reservations and allotments, or to the in-between places in the shifting zone known as the American western frontier in the second half of the nineteenth century, Julius Meyer forged a life and made a living as an American Indian trader, translator and advocate, and eventually as an American Indian curio dealer.

Julius Meyer among his many native friends in front of his "Indian Wigwam" store 1878 in Omaha, Nebraska.

Meyers adventures with the Indians began when on May 30, 1854, President Franklin Pierce signed the Kansas-Nebraska Act, which officially defined the territories of Kansas and Nebraska and opened a significant part of what became known as the "Wild West."

Among the Jews who moved west to settle the land there were many traders and merchants as well as farmers, including the Meyers brothers. In the "Wild West," even those with commercial interests were sometimes part of the great adventure.

Meyer standing next to Red Cloud. L-R seated: Sitting Bull the Oglala, Swift Bear and Spotted Tail. Taken in Omaha in May, 1875. The chiefs he is pictured with were among some of the most important leaders in the history of the west.

Meyers with Lakota Chiefs. His respectful attitude and the per-
sonal interest he took in the tribes, set him apart from many of the
other American settlers. In fact, Meyer's was given the name "Curly-
Headed White Chief with One Tongue." The term "one tongue" was
in honor of his honesty, for a person with one tongue cannot speak
out of two-sides of his mouth.

(above) Meyer interpreting for Iowa Indians, and (below) in a studio shot with tribal leaders.

*Julius Meyer in the 1860's. The natives held him in high esteem,
and he was known among his friends as "Box-ka-re-sha-hash-ta-ka"
meaning "The curly haired white chief with one tongue".*

Julius Meyer pictured in the 1860's, boasted of his close bonds of friendship with Standing Bear, Red Cloud, Sitting Bull, and other Native American leaders whom he paid to pose with him in a series of portraits taken over several years. He became, "a master merchandiser of the Indian to white society."

This is a 1907 picture of Chief Standing Bear, a friend of Julius Meyer. In the 1870s, the government removed the Ponca tribe from their native homelands in northeast Nebraska to Oklahoma. Standing Bear left Oklahoma with a small group but was later arrested by US Army troops from Fort Omaha. Brought to the fort, its commander General Crook was appalled to hear about the conditions in Oklahoma and how the Ponca were forced from their lands. He held a trial in which Standing Bear sued the US government to be seen as a human person with inalienable rights. The court found on the side of Standing Bear, and he was released with his people. He died and was buried there in 1908.

Julius Meyer and Chief Standing Bear

For Meyers there is something of an Oklahoma connection, through Ponca Chief Standing Bear. An article in the September 10, 1926 issue of The American Hebrew read that Julius brought a magician named "Herman the Great" to a Ponca camp to perform for the great Standing Bear and his Ponca people, and how that night as Alexander slept, a young brave attempted to kill him for his hat, believing it to be the source of his mystic power. The Ponca would find their way to Oklahoma after Meyers time.

Standing Bear was Chief of the Ponca, a tribe related to the Omaha, and in time his name would be known for his lawsuit against the United States Army for forcibly removing Indian people from their homelands. The Ponca had tried to deal peacefully with the government and in 1858 signed a treaty giving up all their land except for the land around the Niobrara River in Nebraska. By mistake, the government then gave this land to the Sioux in the 1868 Ft. Laramie Treaty. The Sioux began driving the Ponca off their land.

In 1875 the government admitted its mistake and suggested that the Ponca move to Indian Territory in Oklahoma. Standing Bear and several other Ponca leaders accompanied agents of the Office of Indian Affairs to Oklahoma to pick out a site. The Indian leaders refused all locations finding the arid land uninhabitable. The frustrated agents told Standing Bear that if they wished to return home, they could walk the 500 miles and they did just that.

Upon returning to Nebraska, they found many Ponca had already been moved to Oklahoma. By May of 1877 six hundred Ponca including Standing Bear were forced at bayonet point to walk to the Indian Territory. Several died along the way. After a year in Oklahoma one third of the Ponca had died of disease and starvation, including Standing Bear's son. In the middle of winter Standing Bear led a troop of sixty-six Ponca and set out on foot toward their Nebraska home.

They walked for two months, finally taking shelter on land owned by the Omaha Indians. In the spring the army arrived to force the Ponca to return to Oklahoma. While Standing Bear and the rest Ponca camped outside the town of Omaha the residents of Omaha obtained a writ of habeas corpus on behalf of the Ponca and took the army to federal court.

In his ruling on the case Judge Elmer Dundy ruled, "An Indian is a person within the meaning of the law, and there is no law giving the Army authority to forcibly remove Indians from their lands." The Army ignored the ruling except as it pertained to Standing Bear. His brother Big Snake tried to move from the Ponca Reservation in Oklahoma to one occupied by the Cheyenne Indians.

Indian agent William Whiteman ordered a detail to arrest him. When Big Snake resisted, he was shot and killed. Following a U.S. Senate investigation of Big Snake's death, Standing Bear and some of the Ponca could return to Nebraska. Standing Bear traveled the country telling his story through the Omaha interpreter Susette La Flesche. He died in his homeland along the Niobrara River in 1908. Today there is a Ponca tribe in Oklahoma, and one in Nebraska.

Meyer in his later life was an important member of the Jewish community in Omaha, and when he was found dead in the city's Hanscom Park, with one bullet in his skull and another in his chest, many questions were raised that remain unanswered. Despite a gun never being found and Meyer, who never married, leaving no note, the coroner called his death a suicide. That an observant Jew, to whom suicide is a sin, could shoot himself twice is strikingly unlikely. he left behind a rare trail of photographs from the era, including a photograph of himself with Spotted Tail, Iron Bull, Pawnee Killer, and many other noted chiefs.

Additionally, records state that Meyer was involved with founding both the first synagogue in Nebraska, Congregation of Israel of Omaha (now Temple Israel), and Omaha's Hebrew Benevolent Society, so he was clearly a Jew of faith. When he died in Omaha's Hanscom Park in 1909 at the age of 60 in highly mysterious circumstances, allegedly a suicide, it was reported at the time that he shot himself first in the temple, then in the chest, with his left hand, although Julius was right-handed. Laid to rest in 1909 at Pleasant Hill Jewish Cemetery in Omaha, Meyer was a true man of the frontier, even as he maintained his strong ties to his Jewish identity, a trailblazer who lived during and shaped the exciting times as the Wild West faded into legend.

Solomon Bibo

In 1869, a Jewish teenager reared in Prussia named Solomon Bibo, made his appearance in the small town of Ceboletta, New Mexico, joining two of his older brothers who had already emigrated to the United States. Bibo was born in Brakel, Westphalia, then part of the Kingdom of Prussia, his father was a cantor. Bibo was the sixth of eleven children. Times were tough for Jews in Prussia and many of the sons left for other areas, including the Bibo brothers.

Solomon eventually joined them in the American southwest, moving on October 16, 1869 at age 16. Jews in the Wild West, the Bibo brothers included, often worked as traders and peddlers. The Bibo brothers soon acquired a reputation for fair dealing with the Indians they traded with[28]. Solomon Bibo quickly learned Queresan, the language of the Acoma people, and became involved in their concerns, defending Acoma tribal interests against the aggression of Mexican and American ranchers in the area wanting access and ownership of Indian lands, and against the U.S. Government as well.

Bibo and the Acoma leadership accused the American government of attempting to cheat the Acoma out of their rightfully possessed lands. It came to such difficulties when in 1877, the federal Government offered the Acoma a treaty guaranteeing the tribe 94,000 acres of land in their traditional territory many times that size.

---

[28] Gordon Bronitsky, Ph.D., Solomon Bibo: Jew and Indian at Acoma Pueblo, Southwest Jewish Archives, University of Arizona. Accessed May 14, 2021.

Such a small parcel as the government offered was much smaller than what the tribe felt they should have. The Acoma sought to protect the remaining lands they had. In and effort to do so the tribe in 1884 leased their (communally held) land to Bibo for 30 years. The Acoma got in exchange a yearly payment of $12,000 and the promise that "Bibo would protect the land from squatters, ensure that coal on the tribe's land was mined, and that the tribe would receive the proceeds"[29].

On being informed of the agreement between the Acoma and Bibo, Pedro Sanchez the Indian agent from Santa Fe sent a letter to the Commissioner of Indian Affairs, venting about Bibo, the *"rico Israelito"* (rich Jew), and attempting to have the lease mitigated on the grounds that the Acoma people as a group were not party to the arrangement.

If Sanchez effort had been successful, Bibo was facing not only the revocation hard-won agreement of the Acoma lease, but the revocation of his Indian trading license too! The Acoma quickly came to his defense though, leaders among the Indians circulating a petition with a hundred signatures that was sent to the Bureau of Indian Affairs stating unequivocally the tribal trust in Bibo they all had. In 1885, Solomon Bibo married Juana Valle, the granddaughter of Martin Valle, the Acoma Chief. In that same year, the Acoma elected Solomon Bibo as their new governor.

---

[29] Solomon Bibo (1853-1934), The Jewish Virtual Library, American-Israeli Cooperative Enterprise. Accessed May 14, 2021.

"Don Solomono", as he was known by the tribe, served as in the office four times. The Acoma asked the American officials to recognize Bibo as their tribal leader and, in 1888, he was recognized as such by an agent of the Bureau of Indian Affairs. As the tribal leader with much influence, his pushing for educational and infrastructure reforms brought change and in time resistance. The Indian schools Bibo advocated for were very controversial, sparking unrest between the different generations of the Acoma. He sided against traditional Indians seeking to preserve traditional tribal lifestyles at the pueblo.

In 1889, he aided in having the Bureau of Indian Affairs take into custody and replace a governor who supported tribal members who had used aggressive methods in punishing younger members for following the "progressive" ways taught in the schools. Soon hard feelings developed and because of these increasing tensions surrounding the "progressive" changes Bibo had advocated for, and as well because he wanted his children to receive a Jewish education, Bibo and his family relocated to San Francisco, California in 1898

Juana his Indian wife herself had adopted a Jewish lifestyle and in time converted to Judaism. Solomon Bibo died on May 4, 1934 and Juana in March 1941. They were cremated and interred in the cemetery of Temple Emanu-El in Colma, California. Some of their six children, four girls and two boys, returned in later years to New Mexico and many of the descendants of Solomon Bibo and his brothers still reside in the state among the Jews, Hispanics, and Indians of the area[30].

---

[30] Sandra Lea Rollins, Solomon Bibo, Jewish Indian Chief, Western States Jewish History, Volume #1, Issue #4, July 1969. Accessed May 14, 2021.

(Above) Solomon Bibo as Governor of Acoma

This 1885 photo is listed as "Solomon Bibo governor of Acoma &
his officers 1885 – 1886". Solomon is marked as #15.

Wolf Kalisher

Wolf Kalisher, like Solomon Bibo, would come to be remembered as a friend of the Indian. He was born in Poland in 1826 and moved to Los Angeles, California, becoming a United States citizen in 1855. After the close of the Civil War, Kalisher partnered with Henry Wartenberg in a tannery, one of the city's first such factories. Kalisher quickly became a friend and advocate of the areas Indians, going out of his way to hire Native American workers and defending Indian people's rights as local authorities sought to wrest control of their lives and lands from them.

Kalisher would develop a close friendship with Manuel Olegario, a leader of the local Temecula tribe, advising and assisting the Chief as he campaigned to reclaim a leadership position he had been challenged on, and helped the then restored leader to protect his tribe's land in San Diego County. Kalisher also became an important member of the developing Los Angeles area Jewish community. He and his wife Louise raised their four children in the city and helped establish one of the city's first synagogues. Kalisher Street in Los Angeles memorializes Wolf Kalisher and his efforts on behalf of Native Americans to this day.

Wolf Kalisher[31] was born in Russian-occupied Poland in 1826 and received his American citizenship papers in Los Angeles in 1855. As a merchant, he was noted for hiring local Indians as workers and household help, and for helping the Indians with their disputes.

[31] Doheny Memorial Library, Los Angeles, CA 90089-0189

Louis Wolf

Louis Wolf was another Jew who operated in California's Indian country, like Wolf Kalisher. He was born in Alsace, France on July 27, 1833. Like other Jews who worked in such areas, his efforts are nearly unknown to many today yet are important to America's Jewish history. In his time and place of turn of the century the San Diego County California, he was a unique person, and his life reflects the many ambiguities of life on the frontiers.

According to what was published by the Historical Society of Southern California in 1883 he journeyed by ship from France to San Francisco, arriving by sea in the summer of 1852. He tried to make his way in many areas, working at mining at first like many did. In 1857 he arrived in the Temecula area and began to work as a general merchandiser as well as working cattle on the side; on his passing in 1887 one San Diego publication noted his enterprising personality. Wolf started *"with scarcely any capital but brawn and brain, [yet] he succeeded by dint of industry and perseverance in amassing what is said to be a snug little fortune,"* the newspaper article said.

Another said, "he began a trading business with the Temecula Indians in a small adobe store". His social situation and economic ventures as a merchandiser, cattleman and as an ally to and representative of the local Indian communities was a pattern found among many Jewish entrepreneurs in the remote communities of the West.

Louis Wolf's Store

In 1862, Louis Wolf married Ramona Place, a mixed-race woman who had been born in Santa Barbara in 1846[32]. In the federal census of Santa Barbara for 1850, her father, William Place, was listed as a "Mulatto". He worked as a cook and was born in New York. In the California state census of 1852, her father was enumerated as a "Mulatto", and as having been born on the Caribbean island of Saint Vincent. On the 1860 census for Temecula Township, the Place family are listed as Indians. It is possible that William Place had adopted his wife's (nee Maria Place) family name. There is evidence indicating that Ramona Wolf was of Mulatto and Indian ancestry.

The Indian people of the valley came to know Louis Wolf and out of respect he was known as the "King of Temecula," according to Mrs. Joseph Stillman in an interview on June 13, 1974, when she stated her grandfather, William Veal, had married Isabel Place, Louis Wolfs sister-in-law. Mrs. Stillman said that it seemed likely "that Louis Wolf and my grandfather were Jewish".

---

[32] Wallace W. Elliott, History of San Bernardino and San Diego Counties (San Francisco, 1883; reprint edition, Riverside, 1965), p. 200

In 1845 Governor Pio Pico had granted the Little Temecula Rancho to Pablo Apis, chief of the Luiseno Indians. When this grant was considered for verification before the Federal Land Commission in 1852, the commissioners denied the Indians claim. On January 5, 1852, the Treaty of Temecula was signed by the Native Americans and Federal agent Oliver M. Wozencraft, stipulating that the natives would receive a reservation with livestock and other benefits, but on July 8, 1852, the Senate in Washington DC refused to ratify the treaty. The resulting situation for the Indians was desperate. The Apis grant rejection and the failure of the treaty to get federal Senate approval forced the Indians into being squatters in the valley where their ancestors had lived for hundreds of years[33].

Indian Agent William G. Dryden arrived to disburse $500 of blankets and other supplies that were supplied by the federal Government for the Indians, and much like the Acoma had done with Solomon Bibo in the 1880's when dealing with outsiders, the Indians chose Wolf as their leader to help them negotiate to try and get the message across of their circumstances, which were not good.

With a tribal council called, Mr. Dryden as a representative of the federal government met with them, with Louis Wolf acting as interpreter and at least on a temporary basis as Chief, since Olegario, the tribes usual leader in Washington DC to secure more provisions for the tribe.

---

[33] Van Horn, "Tempting Temecula," passim; Horace Parker, The Treaty of Temecula, passim.

Wolf wasn't what one would call as observant Jew as his biographical data indicates; he was not typical of many of the Jews in the far West in that late 1800's who though far from the institutions of the Jewish community often still maintain some degree of observance of Jewish Law. His connections with the Jewish community of his forebears had been mostly cast aside in the establishing of a new life in California and he had married outside of the Jewish faith. In several other ways as well, his was the experience of many Jews in small southwestern communities where they oft were retail merchants doing business with a wide variety of people, usually involved with livestock ranching and dabbling in real estate.

Many were involved in community affairs and in politics. Like Wolf, many "served as postmasters, justices of the Peace, on school boards". Just as Jews like Solomon Bibo of nineteenth century New Mexico, Wolf Kalish of California, and others, many Jewish men across the frontiers served as a "cultural bridge" between the Native Americans, Hispanics, and the Anglo-Americans, helping to enable a "peaceful mingling" to take place, as William Parish stated[34]. Wolfs close relationship with the local natives, his engagement as an agent for their efforts to gain work helped both parties. It is clear the trusting relations the Indian people of the valley felt for Wolf through their tribal decision to have him act as a (temporary) spokesman.

---

[34] 2 William J. Parish, "The German Jew and the Commercial Revolution in Territorial New Mexico 1850-1900," New Mexico Historical Review, XXXV (April 1960), 132, 141, and pas

This trust they displayed reveal Wolf as someone empathetic to the underdog and aware of the difficulties faced by Native Americans. At least eight children were born to Ramona and Louis Wolf during their many years together, including Henry, William, Charles, Albert, Mamie, Richard, Minetta and Louis, yet there are no known descendants today according to the 1978 interview with a Mrs. Stillman. Louis Wolf died on September 13, 1887 and was buried in an above-ground, brick sepulcher not far from his adobe store.

This store, an area landmark for a century and a half since it was built in the 1850's, served for six decades as part of the headquarters of the Vail Cattle ranch, and in 2015 was renovated and restored as the important landmark it is. The impact of the family on the local area community and especially its Native Americans is recounted today, and in the estimation of many Louis Wolf remains the "King of Temecula".

Louis and Ramona Wolf

Jews and the Indian Territory

The history we have seen so far reveals that even while Indians were in their original territories there were some contacts with Jews who sought through their relationships to better their lives and in many cases, those of the Native Americans with whom they traded. Its an ironic twist in history that some of those same tribes would wind up resettled together in Indian Territory, which became incorporated into the state of Oklahoma in 1907. These tribes were all displaced, as were many of the Jews whose families found their way into the Indian Country that would become Oklahoma in 1907.

Due to the history of the state Oklahoma, Jewish families were less numerous during the days of the Indian territory though they were present but with the allotment of Indians lands in the late 1800's and the arrival of state hood that would change. The Indian nations after they were forcibly removed from the southeast during the 1800's, tribes like the Cherokee, Creek and others, had for generations had limited interactions with Jewish Indian traders, and this continued after their (forced) resettlement west of the Mississippi.

As in other regions, Jews in the Indian Territory were for the most part peddlers who traded with the native tribes. One of the first was Beauregard "Boggy" Johnson. He settled to trade with the local Chickasaw people at what became Boggy Depot in 1865, in time marrying a Chickasaw woman.

As was the practice in the old southeast as well, we find that other early Jewish peddlers in the Indian Territory also married Indian women, especially since at that time it was the means for them to own real estate on reservation Indian lands. Indian Territory would be another chapter in book of the enterprising Jews who would make their fortunes on the frontier, men such as Joseph Sondheimer, who by supplying Fort Gibson for the Union Army during the Civil War, would get to know enough about the area that after the conflict he would be set up to establish a thriving trade with the local tribes. His trading post would do brisk business, his warehouse becoming a well-stocked fur and hide trading site, and the nucleus of what would become the town of Muskogee.

Born on September 22, 1840, in Bavaria, Sondheimer was a boy of twelve when his family arrived in Maryland. As an adult he settled in St. Louis, Missouri, in the years before the Civil War. As the war raged, he would organize commissaries for Union soldiers. After the conflict ended, he soon founded a hide, fur, and pecan enterprise, establishing distribution and shipping depots along the old military road that led from Kansas through the Indian Territory to Texas.

Among the several he established one would be the future site of Muskogee, in the Creek Nation. In 1866 he married Johanna and soon the couple were blessed with two sons, Alexander, and Samuel. The Missouri, Kansas and Texas (MK&T) Railway got rail access in 1872 through the Creek Nation, which opened the area considerably to new business opportunity for the enterprising.

With such opportunity to be had, Sondheimer and family relocated permanently to Muskogee and he made it a central buying site for the pelts he purchased, processed. and shipped back east. He would do well in the years to come, as an article reported in 1892 in the Muskogee Phoenix reported. It stated that Sondheimer handled four-fifths of the hides and furs produced in the entire Indian Territory, which were shipped across the nation and around the globe.

Among what became many Jewish entrepreneurs operating in the Indian Territory, his success amongst them was far reaching, and his life shaped what Muskogee would become immensely; as a member of the chamber of commerce, he invested in the First National Bank, the Oklahoma and Cherokee Central Railroad, and other financial ventures in northeastern Oklahoma.

Joseph Sondheimer, a founder of Muskogee Oklahoma

During his life he was a member of Congregation Beth Ahaba in Muskogee as well as the Benevolent and Protective Order of Elks, and he passed away on July 10, 1913, in Muskogee.

(Above) Beth Ahaba's first synagogue, Muskogee

Laid to rest in Mount Sinai Cemetery in St. Louis, Missouri, his sons carried on the family businesses (Tobias, 1980). Samuel Sondheimer, son of Joseph and inheritor of the family business, described early Muskogee in the Southwest Jewish Chronicle.

> *"This was a wild town. There were no railways, no electric lights and no water. Water was bought by the barrel, and we used candles and lamps for light."*

The Indian Territory days would lure many Jews to the area, with many of the Jewish pioneers arriving in there coming from the same areas of Eastern Europe, leaving political and economic repression for the better prospects of the wild, unsettled frontier among the Indians.

In 1870, Adolph Kohn was captured by the Apache while herding sheep in northern Texas[35], and later was traded to a Comanche living in Indian Territory. He allegedly rode the warpath with them for three years before his release in 1873.

Johnson and Kohn are examples of the many Jews, rugged individuals who carved their own path, with little ties with their religion and ethnicity, making lives and relationships in a tough and tumultuous territory, but such men were atypical, as many Jews would strive to create communities of their own people.

Many Jewish settlers who migrated to Indian Territory and established families and businesses in promising areas sought futures that preserved their identity, as well as promoted community and advanced economic development. A growing number of Jewish families settled in the area in the 1880s after the Territory was linked by the Missouri, Kansas, and Texas Railroad to the outside. Between 1889 and 1895, the United States opened the western parts of its territory to colonists by holding a half dozen land runs.

Non-Indian settlement in the area did not begin in earnest until the great land run of 1889, an event that would draw pioneers and enterprising entrepreneurs looking for opportunity and free homesteads. A small number of Jews too would at noon on April 22, 1889, join the race for "free" land. It was a day of chaos, excitement, and utter confusion.

---

[35] "Roy Davis Holt: An Inventory of His Papers". 1870-1987 and undated. Southwest Collection/Special Collections Library.

Men and women rushed to claim homesteads or to purchase lots in one of the many new towns that sprang into existence overnight. An estimated eleven thousand agricultural homesteads were claimed in a span of a few days.

Land Runs Created Towns Overnight as Indian lands were seized and sold off.

Among the enterprising individuals seeking opportunity in the fray was Moses Weinberger. He was originally from Hungary and found himself waiting in line with hundreds of others to formalize their claims at the territory's official land office in Guthrie. In time he would open Guthrie's first legal saloon, becoming one of the territorial capital's most prominent businessmen.

Boom followed the land runs of the late 1880s, with quite a few Jewish communities soon developing as immigrants to Ardmore, Muskogee, and Oklahoma City married, had families, and a thriving Jewish community developed across the state as it evolved from a frontier.

Jewish owned businesses opened and towns such as Guthrie, Lawton, Enid, Sapulpa, and Apache would see general stores owned by Jewish merchants, as well as their efforts at stablishing other types of stores, diners, tailor shops, and bakeries. Since the steadily increasing number of settlements of the Indian Territory and subsequently Oklahoma was for the most part new, there had not been time for a cemented social stratum to congeal, something that has been repeated throughout the American frontier experience since the colonial days, giving Jews a chance to put their enterprising skills to use.

On the dusty streets of the boom towns, those seeking opportunity there were first judged on their abilities and for what they contributed, not who they were or the ethnicity religion they adhered to, and significant numbers of Oklahoma Jews dove into the political and social life of their new communities, with several becoming Mayors. As the number of Jews in Oklahoma began to grow, they had little established traditions and convention, their Jewish identities survival would depend on the establishing the critical institutions to strengthen their situation and preserve their heritage for future generations in the new "sooner state" that was evolving.

The establishment of the congregation, a foundation of Jewish communities worldwide, was the next step in securing the religious, educational, and social requirements that would allow their communities to thrive going forward, and so the earliest Jewish congregation in Oklahoma was established in Ardmore in 1890, even as the land runs were underway.

Ardmore had about 50 Jews living in the community and these hardy settlers founded the first known organized Jewish community, holding store front services in town at first and twenty-two years later buying their first synagogue, the vacant First Christian Church. The re-consecrated the building was renamed Temple Emeth.

Former church that became Temple Emeth's first synagogue. Photo courtesy of McGalliard Collection at the Ardmore Public Library. Temple Emeth was the oldest congregation in Oklahoma, prior to its dissolution in 2004. According to an encyclopedia entry from the Institute for Southern Jewish Life in 2014, Ardmore's Jewish population has shrunk to two people in this once distinctly Yiddish-flavored town.

Moses Weinberger (center) in front of his saloon in Guthrie

Temple Emeth was a community that would serve its Jewish peoples spiritual needs for over one hundred years. Later, Jews founded congregations in Oklahoma City (1903), Guthrie (1906), Enid (1909), Muskogee (1910), Tulsa (1914), Chickasha (1915), Hartshorne (1916), and Sapulpa (1916) according to sources[36]. Oklahoma City, Muskogee, and Tulsa, each of which had two congregations, would see long lived congregations established and thrive, but many of the other smaller communities with their small-town congregations would see decline as the urbanization of Jews in the mid-20th century led to many of them closing.

---

[36] "From Shtetl to Sooner State: Celebrating Oklahoma's Jewish History." Musenews. 8 Sep. 2009. Exhibit in the sherwin Miller Museum of Jewish Art <http://www.okmuse-news.org/sites/oma/uploads/documnets/2007WinterNewsletter.pdf>.

But during the late 1800's and early 1900's, enterprising Jews had settled in small towns throughout Oklahoma, often opening retail stores. According to research Sam Daube and Max Westheimer established a department store in Ardmore in 1888 that soon became the largest mercantile operation in the city, and in 1896 Jake Katz established a successful store in Stillwater, with his brothers later opening branches of the stores in Pawnee, Sapulpa, and in Ada.

The Froug and Smulian families moved to Oklahoma in 1898 and in time started a chain of The Leader Stores in the booming oil field settlements of Stroud, Sapulpa, Bristow, Prague, Shawnee, Seminole, and Chandler. In Chickasha, cousins Charles Miller and Ben Levine opened the Dixie Store in 1919, which was a well patronized site in downtown until it closed in 1994.

According to research by the Institute of Southern Jewish Life, Sam and Sadie Lee opened a men's wear store in Ponca City in 1914, which was continued by their son Nathan until he closed it in 1998.

Brothers Max and Harry Madansky came to Tulsa from Illinois just after statehood, and in 1908 they started a men's clothing store that in time would have branches in Bartlesville, Muskogee, and Oklahoma City, and in the 1920's this family would Americanize their name to "May". Jewish immigrants continued to thrive in Oklahoma. By 1890, Ardmore, Oklahoma had about 50 Jews living in the community.

(above) Jewish owned grocery store in Ardmore Oklahoma 1920

They founded the first organized Jewish community and began to host occasional store front services in town. Twenty-two years later the Jewish community of Ardmore purchased their first synagogue, the vacant First Christian Church. The re-consecrated the building was renamed Temple Emeth. Oil discoveries would change the face of the new state of Oklahoma, and Jews would play their part with dozens of Jewish owned businesses finding success, which in many cases saw funds going onto strengthening Jewish communities and institutions. The oil boom helped lead Jews to establish new congregations in Okmulgee (1923), McAlester (1934), Seminole (1946), and Ponca City (1962).

By 1937, 7,300 Jews lived in Oklahoma, with over two-thirds residing in either Tulsa or Oklahoma City and the remaining population scattered in smaller cities and towns, primarily in the eastern half of the state. The early 20th century would see many successful Jewish businesses flourish, but changing demographics would lead to the closing, consolidation, or selling of most of them after many decades in the 1980's, 90's and into the new century.

Oklahoma Jewry, small though it has been, has participated significantly in the development of every aspect of the state's life. Jews were representatives in the first territorial legislature. There were also Jews in the convention which decided that the Indian Territory and Oklahoma Territory should enter the Union as a single state. Several Jews served in the state legislature through the years. The Jewish communities in the state have seen increasing urbanization in Tulsa and OKC in recent decades, with the closing of smaller congregations as a result.

In recent years, the Oklahoma Jewish population has shrunk significantly, dropping from 6,900 Jews in 1984 to 4,700 in 2011. While Oklahoma City's Jewish community has remained steady at 2,500 people over the last thirty years, Tulsa's has diminished, declining from 2,900 Jews in 1984 to about 2,000 in 2012. Jewish Oklahomans have always been active in civic and cultural affairs.

(above) Max Weitzenhoffer's father, Oklahoma circa 1913. Max Weitzenhoffer is a longtime producer and London theater owner whose producing ventures include "Dracula" with Frank Langella, "The Will Rogers Follies," and a revival of "A Little Night Music" that brought Catherine Zeta-Jones to Broadway, as well as chairman of Nimax Theatres with his British partner, Nica Burns. They own and manage six West End houses, including the Palace, Lyric, Apollo, Garrick, Vaudeville and Duchess theaters.

In recent years, the once many Oklahoma small Jewish communities have shrunk, with several congregations and their synagogues closing. Ardmore's congregation disbanded in 2003, while Muskogee, which once had two synagogues, saw its last congregation close its doors in 2011. As of 2012, active congregations in Oklahoma were limited to Ponca City, Seminole, Oklahoma City, and Tulsa.

The rich heritage of these Jewish communities and the role they once played in the tumultuous frontier towns of the Indian Territory, Oklahoma Territory and eventually the state of Oklahoma is a testament to the drive and enterprising nature of the Jewish pioneers whose legacy we share. In the state today, there are dozens of families who share Native American and Jewish heritage originating from the early days of the meeting of these two unique communities on the frontier.

Indians and Judaism in the 21st Century

Peru's mainstream Jewish community mirrors many across the diaspora, for the most part urban, well-educated, middle-class, and business-oriented, and mostly descendants of European Ashkenazi Jews. Yet Peru is also home to a small number of devout so-called "Inca Jews", Native Americans from the Andean highlands who were converted by a disillusioned Catholic, and who since have clung fiercely to their identification with the People Israel.

As unlikely and astounding as the long history of Indian and Jewish relations we have looked at in this book so far is, our modern times offers some strange crossroads of race, religion, and culture that are no less surprising, such as how Inca Indians became Jewish settlers in Israel?

While there is no current consensus of the group's members who remain in Peru, an estimated 200 indigenous converts live in two cities that lie 400 miles north of Lima, Peru's capital, and home to its traditional community of around 3,000 Jews. The majority have made aliyah, mostly to the West Bank, where they number around 500.

The B'nai Moshe (Hebrew: בני משה, "Children of Moses"), are from the city of Trujillo, Peru, to the north of the capital city Lima. Judaism moved to the south into Arequipa and to others populated cities like Piura. Most B'nai Moshe now live in the West Bank, mostly in Kfar Tapuach along with Yemenite Jews, Russian Jews, and others.

The community was founded nearly 80 years ago in the mid 1960's by a local man of Trujillo named Villanueva, who faced great exclusion and prejudice in his native city because of his decision to convert from the Catholic Church to Judaism.

Sigundo Villanueva was an Inca Indian who had been a religious Catholic from Cajamarca, the Andean city where Spanish colonialists famously defeated Atahualpa, an Inca ruler, in 1553, would be the catalyst of change for his people.

(above) Jose Urquiza prays in Hebrew at home in Milagros, a particularly impoverished section of Trujillo, Peru, while his family watches. The Urquizas are among the last remaining practitioners of Judaism in Milagros, the former neighborhood of Segundo Villanueva.

Villanueva had in his travels visited Spain for a time, learning from the local Sephardic Jewish community, and in returning to Peru taught around 500 former Catholics in Trujillo about Judaism, igniting a spark which would ultimately lead to their conversion to Judaism and joining the Jewish people as a group. The Inca Jews as a community experienced a long hard road to their eventual relocation to Israel though, since as a group they were mostly rural farmers with no knowledge of Jewish custom and ritual, but they began to practice an iconoclastic form of Judaism in the 1950s among themselves, inspired, they said, by the Psalms. They ate only fruits, vegetables, and fish with scales. Unable to attract the attention of the mainstream Jewish community, they read from a homemade Torah scroll. They prayed wearing homemade prayer shawls. They used the sea as a ritual bath, and the men traveled to Lima to be circumcised.

In obscurity, the group who became B'nai Moshe were practicing Orthodox Judaism to the best of their understanding and abilities, but lacking established contacts in the Jewish world, the new Jewish adherents had to improvise. Many made shofarot and tallisim by hand. One of Villanuevas' followers photocopied every page of the Chumash (five books of the Torah plus haftarah) onto parchment and stitched the pages together to make Torah scrolls[37]. For some 30 years, the Jewish mainstream ignored the B'nai Moshe. Eventually they were "discovered" and examined by an Israeli-led religious court.

---

[37] http://www.scatteredamongthenations.org/peru

In 1985, Villanueva contacted the Lubavitcher Rebbe, who sent Rabbi Myron Zuber to Peru to help with their formal conversions. In 1988, Zuber arrived in Peru and aided the converts in matters such as how to properly observe kashrut and Shabbat[38]. In time their commitment impressed the rabbis and because of the Lima community's continuing reluctance, it was eventually decided that the B'nai Moshe could not reach their full potential in Peru and decided that they make aliyah (emigration) to Israel once converted.

A Beit Din initially performed formal conversions for about 300 members of the community in 1991, almost all of whom soon emigrated to Israel, followed by an additional 200 several years later. When a delegation of rabbis travelled to Lima to formerly convert the group of South American Indians to Judaism, they added just one condition: come and live with us in Israel. As soon as these new Jews arrived in the country, they were bussed straight to settlements in the disputed territories. An interview from Zionism and the Quest for Justice in the Holy Land with Nachshon Ben-Haim, formerly Pedro Mendosa, reveals much about the Indians now Israeli people's view of their journey.

> *"We are of Indian origin, but in Peru, in the Andes, there is no Indian culture left. Everyone has become Christian, and before we became Jews, we also were Christians who went to church."*

---

[38] https://www.shavei.org/communities/inca-jews/

The driving authority of the creation of this community of new Jews being able to make aliyah has been thanks to the chief rabbinate of Israel. At the order of the Ashkenazi chief rabbi, Israel Meir Lau, a delegation of rabbis travelled to Peru and during their two weeks in the country, they converted many people to Judaism, most of them of Indian origin.

> *"We found a small river between Trujillo and Cajamarca and everyone immersed in it. We took the people from Lima to be immersed in the ocean and then we also had to re-marry them all in a Jewish ceremony according to the halakha."*

(Above) Yehudit Jaksa, a member of the B'nei Moshe from Peru now living in Israel.

Helping the Indians become Jews correctly was important to Rabbi Eliyahu Birnbaum, a judge in the conversion court and a member of the delegation, as their right to aliya depended on it. The rabbis converted only those who said they were willing to emigrate to Israel immediately. The Inca Jews like other faced discrimination against native Indians common across South America and had been rejected by the Jewish community in Lima.

"The community in Lima consists of a certain socio-economic class and did not want them because they are from a lower level," said Rabbi Eliyahu Birnbaum, who travelled to Peru a decade ago to convert 90 native Indians. Rabbi David Mamo, the deputy president of the conversion court view of the likelihood for success by the Indians to becoming Jewish was optimistic.

> *"We laid down that condition because in the remote areas where they live, there is no possibility of keeping kosher and it was important for us to ensure that they would live in a Jewish environment. In fact, there was no need for the condition because they were in any case imbued with a love of the land of Israel in a way that is hard to describe."*

Rabbi Eliyahu Birnbaum, as he got to know the members of the B'nai Moshe, was impressed by the Indians commitment to Israel, their passion for Judaism, and their willingness to relocate their entire lives in the name of their faith.

"Because we saw their enthusiasm for the land of Israel, we understood that conversion was part of a complete process including aliyah [immigration to Israel], so we told them: just as you live in a community here, you should join a community in Israel, too," Rabbi Mamo and I both live in Gush Etzion [a group of settlements south of Bethlehem] and we believe that when it comes to community-oriented settlements, there are none that can compare with Alon Shvut and Karmei Tzur [both in Gush Etzion], which said they would be willing to absorb the new immigrants."

On arrival, the 90 new immigrants, comprising 18 families, were taken straight from the airport to the two settlements. Leah Golan, director of the Jewish Agency department responsible for immigration, says:

"We, as the Jewish Agency, bring to Israel anyone who has been defined as being entitled to aliyah - that is, anyone who has been recognized as a Jew by the chief rabbinate or the interior ministry. Generally, the potential immigrants are in touch with our aliyah emissaries and are given very reliable information about housing, employment, and education possibilities in Israel. But in Peru, we do not have an emissary: there is only a small Jewish community of about 3,000 people there, so we only have an office in Lima that is staffed by a local woman.

> *Therefore, the Jewish Agency was not involved in any way in the decision about where these new immigrants would live or what kind of work they would do. All the decisions on those subjects were apparently made by the rabbis."*

Theoretically, the new Jews had the option of joining the Jewish community in Peru, but that was ruled out. "How can I put it without hurting anyone?" Birnbaum says.

> *"The community in Lima consists of a certain socio-economic class and did not want them because they are from a lower level. There was a kind of agreement that if they were converted, they would not join the Lima community, so there was no choice but to lay down the condition that they immigrate to Israel."*

Most of the Inca Jews today live in the West Bank, where they have taken Hebrew names and assimilated well since their resettlement. Some working on farms, and many have joined the Israeli army. Their roots, however, remain important to them as a community.

"We are of Indian origin," Nachshon Ben-Haim, who lives in the Alon Shvut settlement, told Ha'aretz in 2002. The new Jews have been integrated smoothly, with a second generation of the community know growing up in Israel far from the high Andes of their Inca Indian ancestors.

The experience of Luis Aguilar and his family is emblematic of a common experience for the Inca Jews in their exodus to the promised land. Luis, an engineer, became interested in Judaism after the Six Day War in 1967, when he read Theodore Herzl's **The Jewish State**. *"We had never met a rabbi or a Jew,"* Luis recalled, *"but we became very emotional reading this book."* Once the Aguilars were exposed to Jewish practice, they waited for a decade to convert so, in Luis' words, they *"could go to Israel and live as Jews."*

During their decade in limbo, Luis' family suffered severe economic hardship because of the family's steadfast Jewish observance, as Peru is still a very Catholic society. As he explained, *"Aside from the fact that there is little work in Peru, when an employee puts conditions on the employer, he is thrown to the street."* Observing Shabbat was not easy in such a situation.

In Luis' case, his "conditions" were that refused to work on Shabbat or major Jewish holidays. Finally, in November 2001, Luis Aguilar and his family were formally converted to Judaism. They fulfilled their dream of making Aliyah in May 2002. Today, Luis and his family do not have to choose between religious observance and gainful employment, and they are today seeing the results of their decision to make Aliyah as a new generation of their family are now proud sabra (Israel-born) Jews.

(above) Luis Aguilar and his family first studied Jewish texts in this cramped room of their Trujillo home in Peru in 2000 a couple years before the family made Aliyah; (below) Inca Jews at the Kotel.

Afterword

As we have seen through multiple examples throughout this book, since Columbus landed on the shores of this hemisphere, the interactions of Jews and Native Americans has often been a give and take and always a synthesis. In the 21st century, as they have throughout much of their history together in the Americas, Native American and Jews alike have found they have many issues in common; religious rights, resisting assimilation, and the challenge of maintaining language and culture, even while being a part of American and globally connected society, all are pressing for both communities.

As Jews came into close contact with Indians across the moving frontier of American history a reciprocal exchange happened and continues to unfold to this day. From Abraham Mordecai in the old southeast among the Cherokee and Creek in the colonial era 1700's, to Luis Aguilar and his family of Inca Jews today living lives of the modern Israeli Jew, this is a story of shared social experiences of marginalization and tenacious survival to identity. In many cases the two peoples met and across generations blended, as in my own family and thousands of others, bestowing on us a legacy of adventure and enterprise, stoking appreciation for the immigrant and indigenous experience alike. In Oklahoma and across the globe, the synthesis of cultures and peoples is growing, and the syncretism speaks to all people's common humanity and the approach of "The World to Come" rooted in appreciation and understanding of one another.

Index

Bibliography

Bonomi, P. U. (1986). *Under the Cope of Heaven. Religion, Society and Politics in Colonial America.* London: Oxford University Press.

Horowitz, D. (1985). *Ethnic Groups and Conflict.* Berkley: University of California Press.

Koffman, D. (2019). *The Jews' Indian: Colonialism, Pluralism, and Belonging in America.* New Jersey: Rutgers University Press.

Messing, R. A. (1905). "'OLD MORDECAI'—THE FOUNDER OF THE CITY OF MONTGOMERY.". *Publications of the American Jewish Historical Society*, pp. 71–81.

Pickett, A. J. (1900). *The History of Alabama.* Birmingham: The Webb Book Company.

Schwarz, M. (1979). *Cochise Apache Chief.* New York: Chelsea House Publishers.

Tobias, H. J. (1980). *The Jews in Oklahoma.* Norman: University of Oklahoma Press.

Weber, D. (1982). *The Mexican Frontier 1821–1846: The American Southwest under Mexico.* Albuquerque: University of New Mexico Press.

Made in the USA
Monee, IL
10 December 2024

72773090R10072